DARK SHADOWS

DARK SHADOWS
A Domestic Violence Victim

VICKIE RICHARDSON

XULON PRESS

Xulon Press
2301 Lucien Way #415
Maitland, FL 32751
407.339.4217
www.xulonpress.com

© 2022 by Vickie

Contribution by: Kim Johnson & Marvin Richardson

All rights reserved solely by the author. The author guarantees all contents are original and do not infringe upon the legal rights of any other person or work. No part of this book may be reproduced in any form without the permission of the author.

Due to the changing nature of the Internet, if there are any web addresses, links, or URLs included in this manuscript, these may have been altered and may no longer be accessible. The views and opinions shared in this book belong solely to the author and do not necessarily reflect those of the publisher. The publisher therefore disclaims responsibility for the views or opinions expressed within the work.

Unless otherwise indicated, Scripture quotations taken from the King James Version (KJV) – *public domain.*

Paperback ISBN-13: 978-1-66286-536-7
Ebook ISBN-13: 978-1-66286-537-4

This book is dedicated to:

My Children.
My family and friends who were there for me during this tragic event in our lives.
I thank all of them for their concerns, thoughtfulness, and the love they shared with my family during this difficult time of our lives.
There are so many I can thank but, I can't thank them all by name.
God Bless each and every one of them.

*Names have been changed to protect those involved

Acknowledgments

I want to thank my dear friend, Kim Johnson, for taking the time to type and prepare this book for publishing.

Table of Contents

Secret Letter 1

Prelude 3

Domestic Violence 5

Blessings In My Life 7

The Incident 30

Victim 38

In-Laws 41

Call From A Relative 43

Church Appreciation 44

Our Daughters Concern 46

A Mothers Plea For Help 48

Another Crisis To Face 51

Expected Call 54

Surprise Call 59

Lawyer 63

Depressed 65

Counseling 66

Family Visit 68

An Officers Concern 69

Dad's Call 71

Help From A Doctor 78

Back To School 80

A New Nurse....................................81

A Busy Day 82

Medical Blessing................................ 84

Cards 86

Mr. Whalen (My Lawyer) Visits................... 88

Back To Work 89

Dad Calls Again 90

Marvin And Kids Visit........................... 94

Big Night Out (The Wedding) 96

Outside Jail Tour................................ 97

Valentine's Day Cards............................ 99

Bad News Day................................. 101

Valentine's Day Apart........................... 103

Depressed For Sure 108

Mark's Call	109
Pictures	112
Guess Who Called	114
The Truth	121
Verbal Attack	125
Mark Calls Again!	127
Liar	136
First Request	137
Decisions, Decisions	139
Another Call From Dad	142
New Thoughts	154
Court Day	156
My Visit With Mark	158
Signed All	164
Judge Tracy (Impact Statement)	168
Unwanted Thoughts	171
The Big Day	179
Back Home	183
The Last Visit	187
The Night Before	188
The Sentencing 4.9.91	190

Telling The Church............................. 193

The Move 196

It's Over 203

Chillicothe Prison 206

Another Prison Visit............................ 209

Flowers 211

Hocking Hills 212

Court Day For Divorce 213

Still No Answers................................ 214

Thoughts 215

Finally Divorced................................ 217

Counseling Crystal.............................. 218

Visits 219

Sadness 220

Christmas 1991................................. 222

New Year's 1992 225

Letters To Mark................................ 230

Son's Visit 232

16 Months Past 233

Over And Gone 235

A New Beginning 241

Introduction

There comes a time in a person's life when they realize their marriage is at a standpoint. Everything is in shambles. No matter what is said or done the two of you are not happy or in love anymore.

Things that cannot be explained begin to happen. Hang-up phone calls begin, then threatening phone calls start. Late night banging on the walls outside of the house. Light bulbs are being broken. My car is getting egged and spray-painted. These were just the beginning of the downward spiral of my marriage.

The worst was yet to come when the physical attacks began. He began choking me until I could not breathe. Scaring my children while grabbing the steering wheel powerfully while driving. All of these simple, little actions took place beginning in February 1984.

Then, the worst (little did I know) was yet to come. On December 24, 1991 my husband attempted a vicious criminal act in which he was sentenced to seven to fifteen years in prison. (He served nine of those fifteen years). The following chapters are the true story of my life.

Secret Letter

Assumed to have been written by Mark

You have been known for some time now. At first, you appeared to be an all-right person, but I'm not sorry to say that you have become a nuisance and the pushiest person ever.

Others, and I repeat others have wanted to for so long put you straight, but weren't sure how to go about it. That was then.

Your problem is that you try to be a manipulator, persuasive, and influential and in the process, you have been and still are making a pure ass out of yourself. Invest in yourself and save yourself a hell of a lot of embarrassment.

Don't flatter yourself or convince yourself into believing that this is a joke and that this will blow over. Your mouth has finally caught up with you.

We do not know how your kids can put up with you. Your husband has to be admired in order to live with you. Your testimony as a church person is gross. If your church teaches your lifestyle then your pastor needs to learn a few things.

There will be no names put to this letter for good reason. The time is not quite right. You just go ahead and cry to everybody you know. By doing so you are deeply hurting yourself which you'll never be able to get over. You can't stand it when people don't like you and you try to force yourself on them.

Don't take this lightly in the least. This is not a threat. What can be done to you emotionally will be unbearable for you. Don't think that it can't be done. If you knew the authors of this writing that would be more than you could handle alone.

It has been said to let the rat get his self caught with its own trap. Stop before it happens to you.

Prelude

I grew up in the hills of Dry Ridge, Kentucky. As a child, I grew up with a mother who loved me and my sister very much. I grew up learning from her and my grandparents that life was not easy and hard work was necessary. I didn't know my father, he left us when I was three.

I often stayed with my maternal grandparents while my mother worked. I don't remember much about my father being around because he was always gone. My main memory as quoted by my mother is, "The day I was born on June 3rd, 1956 he went to church and I was born in an ambulance on the way to Saint Elizabeth hospital in Covington, KY."

I can't ever remember my father being involved in my life. Nor can I remember my mother even speaking of times about my father being involved with me. Growing up in life without a father was hard. My mother worked two jobs to provide for my sister and our necessities.

After some time passed, I accepted the fact that my father didn't care about my sister and me enough to be involved in our lives. He never tried to contact us, visit, or call. I visited him a few times as a child only to be with my half-brother. After those visits, I had no more contact with my father until my graduation day. He showed up with a picture of my half-brother and some money. I had mixed feelings. I didn't see my father again until the week of my attack, he showed up at my mother's house with money to help me out. I believe this played a role in how I viewed life with my husband and the father of my children.

When I was ten years old my mother remarried. We moved to a house that I thought was a mansion in Hyde Park, Ohio. From age ten and the rest of his life, we called this man "POP". We knew he loved us very much and I truly loved him. He went home to heaven on September 5th, 2018 and I miss him very much.

Domestic Violence

What is domestic violence?
How far should you let it go?
A verbal threat, a slap, a punch, or worst.
When do you decide?
How bad does the violence have to get?
Every situation is different.

During my marriage of fourteen years with Mark, verbal abuse was often. Then the anger episodes. (Anger-James 1:19,20.) (Ephesians 4:31-32).

He would slap me. He liked to throw things. Choked me. Why didn't I leave? For better or worse. The children!

You made your bed you lie in it. What happens in your four walls stays in your four walls. I didn't believe in divorce. Things will get better. He always says", I'm sorry. It will never happen again. But, most likely the abuse will happen again.

None of the above reasons should convict you to stay in an abusive relationship.

Most victims will say,' things aren't that bad. Things do continue being abusive. Most cases are a power play. He's tough, you're not. The abuser wants to dominate you and control your every move.

THE FOLLOWING IS MY STORY!

Blessings in my life

I met Mark in 1971, at a church camp meeting at the age of fifteen. We both were Christians and members of Baptist churches. I immediately fell in love with him. I believed we were meant to be together. Our friendship developed into a long-term relationship of five years. We were married in July of 1976. Here is a story of my many trials that have turned into many blessings.

I was young and in love in 1976. I truly believe I had married the man I was going to spend the rest of my life with. Mark was a faithful Christian man, always attending church with me. I was so sure that he thought the world of me. I was so happy. They say love is blind.....

What I didn't know, was that Mark had many insecurities and tried to dominate me as soon as we married. My love for him closed my eyes and my heart to the problems that were happening around me and would continue to happen over the next fourteen years.

Mark and I started our marriage by eloping in Tennessee. We settled in a small apartment in the western part of Ohio. We were happy. We moved three times to three different apartments within the first two years of our marriage. In 1978, we had our son and named him Seth. The happiness I experienced with the birth of my son was only shadowed by the marital problems as they increased. I began to realize that Mark was jealous of his son. I was innocently giving Seth too much attention and not spending as much time with Mark. To keep our marriage together, I ignored all of our troubles and Mark's volatile attitude, I took one day at a time.

Two years later, in June of 1980, I experienced a miscarriage and lost our second child. At this point in our marriage, I thought I began to see improvement. I was wrong, things only got worse. Our marriage was at a breaking point. Our pastor suggested counseling. So, we went to counseling separately and together. We believed that this was helping we were just kidding ourselves. Ultimately counseling did not help us at all. Realistically, counseling only helps those who help themselves.

We accepted the solution that maybe another child would help our marriage. The Lord blessed us again and in 1982, we had our daughter, Crystal. Mark was so happy; he now has a daughter to spoil. Little did I know that he would eventually end up using her as a weapon to hurt me as well as his four-year-old son. Crystal was his pride and joy. He gave her all his attention, and almost forgot that he even had a son. As years went on, having two children seemed to be causing more problems. I saw our son hurt because he felt forgotten, and was constantly taking the blame for things his sister had done. My heart ached for him. I knew that my children would never be close, because of the turmoil and jealousy that surrounded them in their earlier years.

Years of our marriage passed on. Though we were still being blessed with material things, our marriage became that of two strangers. I often thought of divorce, but I was afraid of the consequences and devastation that my children would have to endure. I felt like we were always on a rollercoaster of fears. I prayed for a solution. I longed for peace and happiness. I settled for being content and accepting my fate, knowing that my trials would bring blessings from God.

In the month of February, our cruelty to each other was so unbearable. Hate was entering into our lives to stay. The pain was driving me crazy. I feel that there is no love left in my life for Mark at all as a husband or as a father.

Mark has now convinced me that there is no love and no want for me at all. Our sex life has stopped. I can't stand to be in the same room with him. He has uprooted my life with our church. He has taken us to churches against our wishes. He has insisted that he will change churches with or without us. Prayer and church are no longer a part of my life as a spiritual woman, which hurts so deeply. That part of me is missing.

Sunday, March 26th, 1989

Mark insisted he would go to Brenda's for Easter dinner with us. I didn't want him to go. On 275 he snapped and terrified us all by grabbing the wheel and causing me to swerve three lanes and almost go in the medium. The kids and I were all frantic. I preceded to drive while shaking and scared. The day was ruined by the decision of what to do. Should I stay or should I go?

When we got home that evening at 9, I left to see Juanita, (A close friend). We agreed I would talk to a lawyer about a restraining order to make him leave for the mental ability and safety of me and my children. I returned home only to deal with Mark's temperament.

Tuesday, March 28th, 1989

I have now made my mind up that I am kicking Mark out on the following Monday, with a restraining order. I have accepted the fact that I can get along independently with my kids. The decision is wrong and hard to do but the road to happiness counts now. I have now realized that our relationship has become so cruel and so unloving. This must be done for all of us. A silent relationship like this can't and won't work.

Wednesday, March 29th, 1989

Mark came home from work and announced that he was going to church with us. The pastor spoke on Hosea taking his wife back even though all she had done. The pastor also called on Mark too close in prayer. His voice got shaky as soon as he said, amen. Mark took the pastor back to his office.

They were there talking for a long time. Finally, the pastor had me and his wife come in. The guilt had finally got to Mark. He admitted he was out of God's will for years. He prayed and asked God and me to forgive him and let him start new. I wanted no part of this. Sunday was the last straw. He had snapped and showed how cruel he could be.

Thursday, March 30th, 1989

Juanita (my friend) convinced me to hold off on the lawyer. I decided to wait and watch Mark until Monday to see how he would react. I have never seen Mark this torn up before. Now he is truly trying to convince me that he wants me and loves me a lot.

I feel I can't handle this.

We have now begun to caress like courting all over again.

Friday, March 31st, 1989

Mark proceeds to tell me he loves me and wants me. I now can't believe how much kindness and gentleness he is showing. Plus, we are communicating with one another through all hours of the night.

Saturday, April 1st, 1989

Mark gets up and goes to get donuts for us.

At 11 a.m. he drops me off at IGA and says he's going to service and he will be back in 30 minutes.

I want him to go get Seth at mom's house without me. He asks me to go, and I go. We stop in to see my grandmother and my dad. At 5 p.m. we get to moms. The brakes went out on the car. Pop has brake fluid. We leave moms at 6 p.m.

Mark cries in the car. Mark then takes Seth to get a slushy and to talk to him. Seth is confused but, he tries to understand the problems.

We put the kids to bed at 10 p.m. We talk at 3 in the morning.

Sunday, April 2nd, 1989

We forgot to set our clocks up so we miss Sunday school. Our friends are coming for dinner. We attend night church. The pastor preaches salvation and living

Blessings in my life

for God. During the invitation, Mark's voice shakes and he goes forward to rededicate his life to the Lord. This surprises the church. In my heart, I hurt, but my mind is glad. I can't cry though.

Our friends come for dinner. We all talk about a lot of different things. Mark breaks down and does a lot of personal talking. He feels so hurt and so bad. I feel so hurt and confused.

Mark tells me that Service Merchandise is holding a ring set he wants me to have. I told him I hope he bought it out of love. Mark keeps telling me that he wants to court me all over again. He tells me he wants to say our vows over again. Just us, the kids, our friends, the pastor, and his wife will attend. This will be when we both feel we are in the deepest love again. Then we will exchange our wedding bands. (This never took place because the verbal abuse started all over again).

This all sounds romantic and exciting to me! I want this to never stop. I just pray to God it's all from the heart. Tonight, I tell him I will let him stay but there are rules he must follow. We will work on love, trust, happiness, and spiritual home!

Monday, April 3rd, 1989

Mark kisses me bye and tells me over and over that he loves me. At 4 p.m. he comes home. I am waiting for him on the swing he tells me he loves me. He takes me to Service Merchandise to fit me for the rings. I couldn't believe the cost. I keep my mouth shut because I don't want to hurt him. He says it's out of love. I stay home from scouts so I can be with him.

We put the kids to bed at 9 p.m. and we talk till 1 in the morning. A LOT of affection is shown. (I wonder if it will last).

Tuesday, April 4th, 1989

Mark is still very emotional about all this. He kissed me bye when he left for work. I was on the porch waiting for him with coffee when he came home. We both need to be alone without the kids a lot. I want to put him first. When we got home, we sit and talk and caress.

We had dinner at 6 p.m. then around 7 p.m. we walked around the block alone, hand and hand. This feels like courting again which I really need. At 8:30 p.m. we went to the bedroom to talk. The communication is great. We are actually talking. Around 9 p.m. my best friend called. Mark was bothered, we talked too long. Mark needs to understand I have calls and friends other than him. I will try to limit them for a while. Phone calls should not disturb him, but he lets his inferiority complex get in the way. We will work on this one too.

At 11 p.m. we laid down to go to sleep. We begin to caress each other. Mark did this out of love without even thinking about the idea of me getting pregnant. I on the other hand feel so confused. I let it happen. If there is still love there, then the hate and the hurt have badly and deeply covered them up. I pray daily about this.

Afterward, we both know we wanted each other. It bothered Mark that I could not tell him I love him yet. I am working on this. Once again, a lot of time and patience will tell. I'll pray about this always.

Those reading this book has to realize that our marriage was an up-and-down roller coaster for most of our fourteen years together.

Wednesday, April 5<u>th</u>, 1989

Mark kissed me bye and said he loved me. He came home from work and my friend was visiting. He was disgusted. I explained she was three hours late. He took Crystal to the gym and went to the dentist.

We talked for a while. He had bad feelings about going to church. He knew he was to go because he rededicated his life to the Lord.

After church, we stayed for men's and women's meetings. He didn't want to but knew he should. We came home and put the kids to bed. At 10:30 we read 1 John 4, a great chapter on love. My friend wanted us to read it. I assume she thought reading this chapter of the Bible would help our marriage.

Thursday, April 6th, 1989

Mark got up and kissed me goodbye. He came home and said he really could not wait to get here. This makes me very happy. Before he never wanted to come home.

At 6 p.m. he walked up to school with me to give the dance teacher her check. I enjoyed this too! He called his friend and made plans to go see him. Then he remembered Seth being gone and wanted to spend the day with me. I told him to go ahead and go so I can learn to trust him again. He needs to go anyway. This would be good for him.

At 8:30 p.m. we walked to Carolyn's house to give her some papers. Mark even stayed for pie and coffee. I am proud of this first step to letting me help him with his complex. We went to bed at 11 p.m. and talked and caressed. I feel that closeness is important to me. I still don't know if there is any love yet but, I'm praying real soon for me to know that there is still real love there.

Friday, April 7th, 1989

I woke up at 5 a.m. and was very sick. I felt like a nervous case of shakes and pains. At 6 a.m. I got sicker and sicker. For once I feel like Mark was very concerned and cared about me. The showing of his love and kindness makes me feel so special. The idea of being pregnant again terrifies me but, if I am it must be God's will.

Mark came home and I went to Sears to get my hair re-permed. I came home and Mark didn't like my hair. This hurts me, but I needed a change. He had made dinner and washed the dishes for me. I love it when he helps out. This shows he cares. I went to bed and fell asleep right away. Mark stayed up later.

Saturday, April 8th, 1989

We got up at 9:30 and I fixed French toast for breakfast. We talked about a lot of things. Crystal has a scout outing in the park at 1 p.m. Mark does not want us to go, this bothers me.

Mark didn't want us to go to a scout outing in the park, so we didn't. He has to realize that I can give the kids time and him too.

Later on, I knew deep in my heart that the mental abuse was going to start all over again.

We went to Forest Fair Mall and had a good time hand in hand. We came home at 1:30 p.m. and lay on the couch until we fell asleep. At 6:30 p.m. Mark went to Kroger's for me. When he got home, we made supper and went to bed.

Sunday, April 9th, 1989

We got up at 7:30 a.m. for church. Home from the church at 1 p.m. and ate dinner. I babysat for my nieces today and went to IGA. I have been on edge today. The kids got on my nerves and I felt bad all weekend. Mark still assures me that he loves me and wants me.

Went to see a dear friend at the nursing home at 5:30 p.m. then went to church at 6 p.m., and home by 7:30 p.m. Dinner is over with! Everett stopped in till 10 p.m. He talked to us about the church and new offices.

We have been too tired to read at bedtime. We need to read every night! The devil keeps fighting to try to win us over. I know we can overcome all of his tricks. The Lord has more power. He will help us a lot. Prayer will make us very happy and fulfilled. My feelings are still confused.

Monday, April 10th, 1989

Up at 6:30 a.m. to kiss Mark goodbye. This is great, I need this! I stayed home today till 1 p.m., then Shonda took me to Friendly's for lunch. I had a crab salad, which I did not like, and a malt. Came home and fell asleep on the couch. Seth woke me up.

Had dinner at 4 p.m. We left at 5 p.m. to visit family. We left the kids with a family member and went to the funeral home of a friend. We picked the children up at 7:30.

Mark is still really down and people at work don't like his attitude. He is rude and not tolerable at all.

Tuesday, April 11th, 1989

Mark kissed me goodbye! My day was full of reading and a visit with my dear friend Carolyn. At 2 p.m. I went to Carolyn's. I then had a conference with my daughters' teacher at 3 p.m., Carolyn had my kids.

Mark and I peddled in the yard. At 6 p.m. we took a walk around the block arm in arm. When we got back, we did the dishes and put the kids to bed by 9 p.m. We sewed together on a backpack putting on Velcro straps for Seth's trip. We had a Bible devotion together reading 1John 4. (I really wanted all of these devotions to continue but in my heart, I knew they would stop.)

My feelings are getting down today. Takes a lot of time and patience. I pray that I see positive events in our marriage and wanted very much to believe that things would be better.

Wednesday, April 12th, 1989

Mark wakes me at 6 a.m. and tells me he is going to work with an attitude of talking a thousand words to everyone there. This bothers me because I hear conceitedness and sarcasm in his voice. I do not like this. I want him to associate with the people he works with, but not like it's a necessity.

Today I am down all day. The devil is working on me. Mark comes home and sits down to eat and the first thing he says is, "I didn't want to come home today." This was an innocent statement but sounded terribly wrong.

We learned today that it is very easy to get frustrated, which leads to anger. We had an argument and neither of us said we were sorry. This hurts because the Bible says to never go to bed with anger on your mind. Of course, this was nothing new for us since this happened a lot of evenings in our fourteen years of marriage.

We went to church and I stayed to help clean. Afterward, we said we were sorry. I hurt a lot because I fear the past. We need to pray about this always.

Thursday, April 13th, 1989

Up at 6:30 a.m. so Mark could tell me bye. I have now begun to tell Mark "I love him again." I am trying to lift all my hurt to love again. (At the same time wondering if this is possible.)

Mark comes home and we do our jobs. He works on the car and I take Seth to get new shoes for his hiking trip. We eat at 6 p.m. and then at 7:30 p.m. I go to a board meeting. There was an incident that caused me to forget my briefcase. Mark went back up to the school to get my case. I was very proud of him because he told the board he would listen to me first, not them. He came back and we talked about the problem. He agreed with me and them too. A board member called to check on me, she cared. I went to bed on Mark's chest upset. I kept waking up off and on all night.

Friday, April 14th, 1989

Up at 6:30 a.m. again. I kiss Mark goodbye. I can't go to work because my car starter is not in. Some of the board members call to talk. My feelings are so badly hurt. They have hurt me.

Finally, at 3 p.m. or so I talk to a friend. We each said a lot of harsh words. We ended the call nicely though. I guess we will start new next week. I feel that sometimes when you are in an abusive relationship to seem to take your problems out on other friends that you care about. Doesn't make it right but we are only human.

Mark came home at 4:30 p.m. He stayed at work and talked for a half hour. We ate and took Seth to Shonda's to go with Jeff. I will miss him. We fixed the car and mowed the lawn. We bought Crystal a new pair of shoes. Then we watched television and went to bed at 11:30 p.m. Our caressing has slowed down a lot! This worries me. Mark bought a tape on relationships which I feel we do not need. God's word should be enough. We did listen to the tapes. I felt that our marriage could use all the help we could get.

Saturday, April 15th, 1989

Mark went to visit his friend.

Seth went with Jeff.

I took Crystal to Jenny's.

I finally had time to myself which I hadn't had for a long time.

At 6:30 p.m. Mark came home.

We went to Hardees to get a sandwich, then to Friendly's to get a Jim Dandy. We took it to Colerain Park to eat it together. We paid to watch a movie and sat in the living room together. We went to bed at 1 a.m.

<u>Sunday, April 16th, 1989</u>

Went to church.

Relaxed all day.

The following week was normal.

On Friday, April 21st we did the yard work together. Mark's work cut his time to four days a week. We aren't worried though; they will make him work overtime soon. Learning this news didn't bother us, because I knew the Lord would provide like he always had.

<u>Saturday, April 22nd, 1989</u>

Mark took Crystal out to eat and to the park.

Seth and I went with Carolyn and Rick to Red Lobster.

Mark took Seth on a bike ride.

Monday, April 24th, 1989

I got up at 7 a.m. with Mark. We walked the kids to school. Then we went to get donuts. Mark went to work with me and helped me. We got finished at 12:15. We came home to take showers. Then we went to bed. It feels good to finally feel loved again.

Mark took Seth to the orthodontics.

We ate at 5 p.m.

We went to the Scout meeting at 7 p.m.

Kids to bed at 9 p.m.

We talked, and it was very upsetting! We talked till midnight. Mark got upset because I told him the reason people don't come around is that he is not associative. People won't come around when they think they are not welcome. They talk to me when Mark is not around. We went to bed angry at one another.

Saturday, May 13th, 1989

We had a bad argument that lasted till 1:30 a.m. I feel Mark doesn't care anymore.

Sunday, May 14th, 1989

Mark's birthday and Mother's Day.
A really lousy day.
Had arguments all day.

I stay frustrated all the time now.
Mark truly doesn't care.

Tuesday, May 16th, 1989

We went to the park and had a picnic. The kids love family picnics.

Wednesday, May 17th, 1989

Mark has come home late from work every day this week. He came home tonight with the statement he was going to another church.

All of June and July were a living nightmare!

Once again, I want to remind my readers that all of these pages of information are leading up to the night of the most tragic event of our marriage.

We took a trip for two days to Amish country for our anniversary. We were trying to work on our relationship, but nothing changed. He also went to get my ring but canceled the set that he promised me and bought a single band instead. I was upset and he didn't care. Please understand, I was so tired of being disappointed in this marriage.

Thursday, August 17th, 1989

Mom came up to stay this past week with me and Shonda. She and Mark and I stayed up till 2 a.m. talking. He told my mom all about our problems, which really upset her. All of this is one hopeless mess.

Wednesday, August 23rd, 1989

Mark came home from work and packed a suitcase. He told the kids he was leaving us.

Crystal was very upset.

Seth quoted him from the Bible.

I just cried.

I wanted him to leave but, the kids talked him into staying.

This was a lot of mental torment put on all of us, especially Seth. Seth was not able to sleep or relax. He is up and down all night. He is disturbed so badly about the problems in our family that he asked his dad to leave. He loves him but he cannot stand the arguing and torment we all seem to face day to day.

September 1989

September has come and school has started. The problems are still here in the family and getting worse. It hurts me so badly to see the effect these marital problems have had on Seth. He used to love to go to church, read his Bible, pray, and love God. Now it's a matter of not caring about any of the religious values he once loved. He has no interest in God's word at all.

He doesn't care about school. He gets depressed about going and doing homework. All of this hurts me deeply, for I now have a scared, very low self-esteemed child. I see no happiness in my son at all. All of this led me to put him on a drug sedative to help him relax and sleep more soundly. I just pray to God that something will change all of this mess. My son needs a good state of mind to be happy!

<u>January 1990</u>

New year same problems! Christmas came and I could not wait to get it over with. For the new year, the kids have asked that Mark and I argue less. We want more happiness, and Mark promises to change. This never happens, just another lie.

<u>Friday, January 12th, 1990</u>

For the first time, I feel the need for a separation. I feel like Mark is messing with my mind, except in a quiet, relaxed, subtle way. I will explain this more later. He is trying to drive me crazy!

Blessings in my life

When my mom visited on the 8th, Mark and she got into a heated argument. They both were wrong and should both apologize to each other. They never will.

This has been a terrible week. My nerves have been really bad. I even break out in hives. A couple of weeks ago Mark left at three in the morning. He is determined to make me think he is having an affair.

Yesterday, on the 11th I found his wedding band in the wash. He hasn't even asked about it. I also came home unexpectedly and found the yellow pages open to lawyers.

Today, I find a paper he wants me to find. A bunch of statements and numbers like a code on them. He's just waiting for me to ask him what it is. Instead, I put a note in his lunch with an extra treat, and he brought it back to me mostly.

He is trying to mentally in a nice way torment me!

Saturday, January 13th, 1990

Today I went down to see one of mark's family members to talk to him about Mark. I wanted them to know how Mark was treating me. He didn't give me much help. He will back me up though.

Sunday, January 14th, 1990

Mark talked to his family member today about our problems. The family member later told me that Mark does want to work it out. Also, for me to be patient and work on it too. He did not know that I work on our problems every day.

At 11:30 p.m. Mark and I went to bed. He pestered me for an hour until finally, I gave in to the lovemaking. Sometimes I have to worry about being pregnant. I'll pray that I'm not. I am sure this will cause great tension between us. We definitely do not need to bring another child into this marriage.

Sunday, August 19th, 1990

At 5:30 I was getting ready for church and Mark physically attacked me.

He choked me.

He slapped me.

Told me he would kill me.

What made him stop the abuse? Crystal walked in and saw so he stopped.

I locked myself in the bathroom and wouldn't come out. Finally, he left with Crystal and attended church as if nothing had happened. Seth was at church already.

Mark went to his family members and told them what he did. At 7 p.m. he went to church to get Seth. He told the pastor, Shonda, Jeff, and the kids.

I was terrified. I called the women's abuse center. They suggested that I get a restraining order against him. I decided not to. I didn't want to keep the kids from him. I ask him to go stay with his family but he wouldn't.

My feelings are all mixed up and also very frightened of him. We will halt all physical touching. The week has gone badly. Not much has been said at all. It will take me a long time to forgive and forget this attack. The Lord will have to deal with this one in his own time.

The next few months dragged on and problems persisted. We are trying to make it work, but I feel it will never change.

The Incident

Sunday, December 23rd, 1990

Our day began with an argument because he wouldn't let Crystal go to church with me. Finally, after enough persuading, he decided to go with us. This frustrated me because once again he caused us to be late to church.

Home from church and the afternoon went pretty smoothly. We left early for evening service so we could visit a friend in the nursing home. Also, Crystal had a Christmas present for Vera Thompson whom we also visited. After church service,e we went to Mark's parent's home because his sister was home from New Jersey. We stayed there until 9:30 p.m. When we got home, I fixed us all something to eat. After dinner Mark and I wrapped the kids' Christmas gifts. During this time there was peace in the family.

At midnight Mark made the kids go to bed. We stayed up doing Christmas things. Mark had asked me for a candle and matches to put in his car. I gave them to him.

He claimed he wanted to use them in case of a weather emergency. It didn't seem weird at the time.

Monday, December 24th, 1990

2 a.m. Christmas Eve morning. Mark asked me to leave the kids and go for a drive with him. I refused to go because I will not leave my children alone at night even while they are asleep. Now that I think about this, I believe in my heart that he was going to take me out and burn me and leave me somewhere. I realize the above statement is only here to say but, these are my true feelings. At about 2:15 a.m. Mark went to bed. Crystal was in our bed also so I stayed up on the couch reading a book. I eventually fell asleep there.

4 a.m. the phone rang and Mark rushed to the kitchen to answer it. This was odd to me because all he had to do was answer the phone in the bedroom. He told me it was the wrong number and that someone was asking for Chad. I once again expected this answer. He came downstairs and sat in the living room chair. We talked about Christmas and New Year's resolutions. For once we were not arguing!! During this conversation, I stated to him that in February that I was going to leave him as soon as I could get a job. We also agreed that until this time we would be married in name only. We could each come and go as we pleased. He asked me if he could leave the house for a while. I told him to go on and leave.

He got up and went into the kitchen and before I knew what happened he was pouring paint thinner on me while I was asleep on the couch. He was carrying a newspaper rolled up that he lit like a torch. I jumped up and struggled, begging him to stop. He kept dousing me with the paint thinner. Then he dropped the can and held me tight and set me on fire. I pleaded with him to stop, but he just ignored my cries. All I could think of was to protect my face and get away.

I was screaming very loudly. Our daughter woke up and this caused him to stop. I do not know if she saw me on fire or not. She told my brother-in-law Jeff later that she did see me. I struggled down the hallway, blinded by the fire, to feel my way to the bathroom. I yelled at my daughter to go into her brother's room and stay there. Finally, I was able to find my way to the tub. I got on my knees and turned on the cold water to put out the fire on my hair and nightgown. I yelled at my kids not to open the door and stay there, and they did.

A few minutes went by, Mark came into the bathroom door to see me. I stood there in shock, crying with much pain, not even knowing how badly I was burnt. I told him to stay away from me and go call my sister Shonda. Much to my surprise, he did! First, he called my sister, then he called 911, and lastly, he called his dad. He waited for the police to come. My brother-in-law came to get the kids.

The ambulance arrived first, then officer Angela Hunan of Colerain Township police. The ambulance took me to Providence hospital and transported me to University Burns Unit.

Newspaper articles from the Northwest Press:

■ CRIME
Husband sentenced for burning wife

Larry D. Gibbs was sentenced to prison Tuesday for dousing his wife, Vicki, with paint thinner and setting her ablaze on Christmas Eve.

Hamilton County Common Pleas Judge Ann Marie Tracey sentenced him to 7-15 years without probation for the first six years.

Saying the attack was "planned and purposeful," Tracey also admonished Gibbs, his family and friends against blaming the victim.

Gibbs, 35, pleaded guilty to felonious assault after prosecutors agreed to dismiss an arson charge.

1-2-91

Man charged with setting wife on fire

A Colerain Township man doused his wife with paint thinner and then set her on fire last week, police said.

Colerain police officer Angela Human said 36-year-old Larry Gibbs, 9669 Crusader Drive, was arrested and charged with aggravated assault in the Christmas Eve incident. Police say other charges are pending in the incident.

According to police, Vickie Gibbs, 24, suffered burns over about 20 percent of her body, mostly to the head, neck and chest area. Police say her husband used a rolled-up piece of paper that he lit as a torch to set her on fire.

Vickie Gibbs was transported to Providence Hospital and then transferred to the University Burn Center.

Her husband pleaded not guilty Dec. 26 in front of Hamilton County Municipal Court Judge Deidre Hair. He is being held at the Hamilton County Justice Center on a $200,000 bond. A preliminary hearing has been set for Jan. 3.

The Incident

> **4-10-91**
> **Spouse sentenced for fiery assault**
> CINCINNATI — Larry Gibbs, 35, who pleaded guilty to throwing paint thinner on his wife and setting her on fire, was given a 7-to-15-year prison sentence Tuesday. Vicki Gibbs, 34, suffered third-degree burns to her chest, arms and face. Hamilton County Common Pleas Judge Ann Marie Tracey imposed the maximum sentence and ordered Gibbs, of Northbrook, to pay court costs of about $7,500. She called the crime "reprehensible."

I have yet to know why and probably never will, but I thank God my children were not hurt and my home was still in place. I am also very thankful my face and the rest of my body were not burnt. I will have to live with mental pain and fear for the rest of my life. I will never understand how a man could claim to love his children, but then, set their mother on fire. He put them in danger and possibly could have destroyed our home and all our belongings. Which God has so graciously blessed our family with.

Now that I think back to when he choked me in August and threatened to kill me, I should have left then. I have tried so hard to keep my marriage together for my kids because my father left when I was three and never cared about me.

About a month before the incident Mark filled the tub with water and stood at the stove playing with the burners. I also believe now that my thoughts at 2 a.m. were right, he was planning on burning me then and changed his mind. My feelings now are of much fear, loneliness, peace, relief, and many unknown answers to so many questions of "why?".

He has hurt my entire family and relatives. Lots of friends, my church, and many people who thought so much of him, and cared for him. This is a man who went to church, served on the PTA board, and played Santa Claus for children just weeks before this. Now my children and I are left with financial burdens. They have to cope with their mother being burned. Also, their father burning me, and him being in jail.

I thank God I have loving relatives, caring friends, and lots of support from my church. They have helped us get through such a tragedy as this.

January 15th, 1991

Today is a new start for me. I have lots of blessings to be so thankful for. I have a church that supports me. I have friends who have helped and supported me as well.

My dear friend Carolyn does my bandage changes for me.

Karen helps me a whole lot.

Terri talks to me and makes me laugh.

My sister gets aggravated with me.

My mom helps me in lots of ways.

My son has never emotionally broken down. He holds in way too much.

The Incident

My daughter talks a lot, says a lot, cries a lot and is real goofy acting. She also says things that she doesn't realize hurts me like:

If daddy was here, I wish he was here and not you, I miss him, I love him, I don't understand, I don't know why, when can dad come home? Why?

My daughter would tell people that a monster burnt me not her dad. (Remember this at that time was a frightened eight-year-old girl who was dealing with all of this emotionally.

Victim

January 14th, 1991

Today I have to testify before the grand jury. This decision was made with the help of my lawyer Mr. Whalen. I was nervous but determined to charge him with the indictments of felonious assault, and aggravated arson. Each of these charges can be punished by 15-25 years in prison. I prayed to the Lord that the following statements and questions asked would be truthful, blunt, and simple.

1:30 p.m.

Prosecutor: Jerry (prosecutor)

Victim: Me

Court Representative: Present

12 Jurors: Present

Prosecutor: "State your full name and spell it."

Me: "Vickie Elaine Gibbs"

Prosecutor: "Where do you live?"

Me: "----, Crusader Dr., Colerain Township."

Prosecutor: "Your husband's name?"

Me: "Mark Gibbs"

Prosecutor: "Does he live with you?"

Me: "Yes"

Prosecutor: "Did he live with you on December 24th, when he hurt you?"

Me: "Yes"

Prosecutor: "tell the jury what happened on December 23rd on Sunday, the proceeding day.

Me: I told the days actions from the Sunday morning argument until he torched me at 4 a.m. the next morning.

Prosecutor: "Has your husband had prior mental help?"

Me: "No, but we have had marriage counseling."

Prosecutor: "Tell me about your children."

Me: "Seth is 12 years old and a straight-A student." "Crystal is 8 and her daddy's little girl."

Prosecutor: "If I was to put Seth on the stand, what would he say?"

Me: "He would tell you that we argued a lot and that he has heard his father threaten me a lot."

Prosecutor: "If I was to put Crystal on the stand what would she say?"

Me: "I would not allow Crystal to testify because she is too immature, confused, and emotionally upset."

Prosecutor: "How do you feel about your husband?"

Me: "I feel that he is not insane, but does need mental help."

Prosecutor: "Does the jury have any questions?"

(No one asked any more questions)

"You may step down."

In-Laws

January 18th, 1991

Tonight, my in-laws did finally show up with our animals and Christmas presents. This was a joy to the children but a hard time for me. My body shook and my words were unsure. I felt so much fear inside. These people have been truly loved by me, and I will always care for them.

My mother-in-law did not say much, but she still insisted that I, the victim, provoked this crime of being a human torch. My father-in-law did not say one word at all. He sat and grinned, making an unknown expression as I begin to tell them the whole story. I told them the truth of what happened from December 23rd at 7:30 a.m. till December 24th at 4 a.m., when the violent act took place. I feel no matter what I say my mother-in-law will always believe that I provoked him even if my words of truth come out in court.

My father-in-law gave the impression, from the looks he expressed, that he knew I was telling the truth. He most likely knew that someday Mark would try to hurt me. No one would have ever believed that he would turn me into a human torch…. LOOK AT MY BURNS!!!

These are real, these scars I can't hide. This is all the proof I need. Sure, my burns will heal completely someday, but mentally, I may never heal. The scars will be there to remind me, I may never understand WHY!! To make matters worse, I will still live with the fear of Mark hurting me again. My in-laws need to realize that even though this is hard to accept, Mark needs to suffer the consequences that the Lord and the courts give him. He should know and accept whatever happens.

Call From a Relative

January 19th, 1991

Finally, a relief of wondering has settled in my mind. A sure surprise. A moment of special love. A Gibbs family member has finally called.

Mark's cousin, has finally felt enough concern for a cousin of 14 years of marriage to call. Her concern was for my injuries, also the children mentally, and if we needed anything. After a pause of crying, I told her how she was the first of Mark's family member to contact me in any way at all. She was even shocked to know that not one of them even sent a get-well card to us.

She tried to explain her feelings, but had a difficult time doing so. She promised to come and see me in the coming weeks. I told her I would like that!

Church Appreciation

<u>A letter to my church</u>

January 20th, 1991

To my brothers and sisters in Christ,

Pastor, I want to say I'm sorry to all of you. For a long time, Mark and I have been a burden to this church. I am sorry. My children and I want to thank all of you for helping us through this trial. Your support and all of your prayers and phone calls have helped us greatly. My children and I love all of you and are graciously thankful for the different ways each of you have helped us.

Please continue to pray for us, and I know God will get us through the new start we have to face. He has already blessed us tremendously, through all of you. We know without all of you we could not deal with this trial. God has blessed us daily in ways I didn't even expect.

To speak of Mark, I would like all of you to pray for him. We may never know why, but God does. Do not feel hatred towards him, please care. A lot of you have known him for years. Remember him as you did then.

> May God bless you all,
> Vickie, Seth, and Crystal

Our Daughter's Concern

Sent to Mark on January 22nd, 1991:

A sweet poem
Sweet, sweet star above
Protect my daddy from above
I hope you send him home alive
Because I love him
With lots of tears
I hope he doesn't stay there long
Because I love him more than ever.
Love, Crystal

P.s. also sent was a painted rainbow, a note of love and being missed, and a picture she drew of a ninja turtle.

Our Daughter's Concern

Dear Vickie:

How are you doing? I know you are going through a lot right now. Bro. Danhof has told me that the church is helping you some financially and I also understand that you are easily receiving quite a bit of help from other sources.

I want you to know that I do not want you to be afraid of me. Please believe me.

Even though the state has picked this up, my prosecution says mostly in your hands. I know that I sent myself here, but it will be the most your past that sends me elsewhere. I don't want the kids taking that you deserve the biggest part in this.

I hope the kids are doing better. Believe me I feel for you and the kids. Renee's little prom was very touching. I shared this with some of my inmates.

Prayer to you may not mean a whole lot right now, but I would like to request that you pray for us.

I'll close for now. I will write you later on if you don't mind. My thoughts are with you and I am concerned. Bye for now.

Love,
Larry

A Mother's Plea for Help

January 21st, 1991

Today began with my nerves really on edge. I found myself getting angry with my children, which needs not to be done. During the early morning hours, one of Mark's family members called me. The following is our conversation as best as I remember:

Family member: "Vickie, you said you cared about me! Well then, please drop the charges against Mark."

Me: "No, it's out of my hands. I will not let him out to hurt me again."

Family member "I guarantee you he won't be around you again."

Me: "No, you can't guarantee me that because nobody knows. He could have hurt your grandchildren and burnt up our home."

A Mother's Plea for Help

Family member: "I know that now you will be happy with him away."

Me: "How can I be happy knowing after 14 years of marriage Mark burnt me? I have to live with my burns and a daily reminder for the rest of my life. I have to deal with my children and my emotional status. My children need counseling.

Family member: "You should have left."

Me: "If he cared about his children, he should have moved in with you but he wouldn't. He wanted me to leave instead. I refused to take my children out of school and uproot them. What he really wanted was full control of my children. He wanted me hurt badly enough so I couldn't care for my children. I have proof that he wanted to kill me and all of this will come out in trial. You will be hurt if all of this goes to trial. I don't want to hurt you. Please try to understand.

    She then started to tell me that Mark and I were always jealous.
    Then I decided to be a little spiteful also, I told her that her and her husband had never been happy either.
    She told me I was not to step on her property anymore and to not speak to her.

Well, I realized the conversation was getting nowhere, so I slammed the phone down.

Then she had Mark's lawyer, Jack Rubenstein, call me.

I told him to call my lawyer, Bill Whalen. He was surprised that Mr. Whalen was representing me. This really gave me feelings of so much hurt to speak to Mark's family member the way I did. She needed to accept reality and realize how serious this tragic incident is.

Another Crisis to Face

January 25th, 1991

I felt humiliation of hard times today. I had to go apply for welfare. I am applying for ADC, Medicaid, and food stamps. My friend Debbie went with me. She drove me there; I am too much on edge to drive to these places of importance.

After having an appointment at 8:30, we still had to wait until 10:30 to be seen by a caseworker. She had us fill out forms, then there were lots of questions to be answered. My frustrations were building up the more we sat there. Finally, after a lot of signatures and a lot of do's and don'ts, we were told the unbelievable words of, "the agency will give you about $330.00 a month, also you will receive food stamps monthly." Then she asked "what will you do?" I told the caseworker I would go home and pray a lot. Then the tears came and I couldn't stop crying.

It is strange, even welfare has a code for Mark. He is considered an absent parent by the code of JP (jail-prison). Through a normal divorce he would have been LS (legally separated), and DI (divorced). This should have been this way, with child visitation rights. I keep telling myself, only he has done this to himself. My fear has to keep him in prison. As hard as this situation was, becoming a welfare applicant was an embarrassment to my 12-year-old son which was just another problem I had to deal with.

> Thankyou for sending the chaplain my way. I had a very nice visit with him.
>
> I understand that you are recieving different kinds of help. For this I am very happy to know.
>
> My thoughts for your well-being goes to you. You can take my apologies however, but I'm sorry for my reactions.
>
> God has been dealing with me in many ways. I am more than willing to take whatever comes my way.
>
> Believe it or not I have appearched many inmates with the Word. A few have been coming to Bible study with me.

Another Crisis to Face

> I do pray every day several times for you and the kids. I am assured that they are doing well.
>
> Take care.
>
> Larry

Expected Call

January 25th, 1991

Here we are! Waiting for a 9 a.m. phone call. Guess who's calling? JP-daddy? At 9 a.m. sharp- ring, ring! Crystal shows lots of joy when speaking to him, but after talking for a while she gets upset. This is supposed to be part of her therapy.

The following are parts of the conversation: (I do screen the calls.)

Crystal: Why did you do this to mommy?

Mark: Well, daddy don't know!

Crystal: You got to know!

Mark: Daddy didn't react right!

Crystal: Why didn't you help her?

Expected Call

Mark: There was nothing I could do she was just in pain.

Crystal: There must be a reason.

Mark: I don't know, it shouldn't have happened this way.

When are you coming to see me?

Crystal: I don't know if I will ever come see you.

Mark: Well, I'll see you soon!

Crystal: No, dad no, not soon! A long time!

Mark: Well, that's okay, isn't it?

(Seth gets on the phone)

Mark: Good to hear your voice

Seth: (not talking)

Mark: How's the comic's coming?

Seth: Fine, I won't send you one for a while because other kids want them.

Mark: That's okay

Are you doing fine?

(Background laughter)

Sounds like everything's back together.

Seth: Yea, well dad I'm going to go now. I love you, bye.

(Seth never has much to say)

Crystal: Dad?

Mark: I'm going to describe a person who came to see me in my next letter. You guess who and write back and tell me.

Crystal: Okay.

Me: Crystal, five more minutes. Tell dad if we aren't home next Friday to call on Saturday. (She did.)

Mark: Mommy will probably stop the phone calls.

Crystal: Is jail fun?

Mark: Crystal, this is important; I'm not terribly upset.

>Your church prays for me.

Expected Call

Your Sunday School teacher prays for me.

I get lots of outside support.

People and preachers come to see me.

God is here with me. I read my Bible.

Me: Crystal, time to hang up.

Seth: Dad, mom says, "call next Saturday!"

Mark: Okay.

Crystal: I'm back!

Mark: Begins to tell her he will be home soon.

Me: This upset me, so I took the phone away and hung up.

Crystal: Mommy, (I'm upset, crying)

She will not understand that I did this for her good. Some day she will though! She has to accept he is not coming home. Excepting phone calls from the jail is supposed to be part of the therapy for the kids. I feel these calls just cause more heartache and explaining that I have to do that I don't have answers to.

Dark Shadows

Some may wonder why I included the children's phone calls with their dad. I want my readers to understand how all of this through their dad's phone calls from jail affected them. This is important.

Surprised Call

January 28th, 1991

My mother came up to stay with me today. This was a good idea because I needed her. I was in a state of depression over the weekend. I feel that I still have not come out of the shock. I wish this tragedy was behind me. I know emotionally I will never be over this.

My surprising phone call was from another one of Mark's family members. He asked, "If he could come and see me?" I said, "yes, as long as he doesn't talk about the court, trial, crime, and all things concerning this awful tragedy." He said, "he just wanted to come and see how me and the kids are doing." I said, "he could come on Wednesday at 5:30 p.m." He said, "OK.

I took my mother to meet my Pop so he could take her home. I came home and tried to be content and alone. Part of me was sad. Because now I would be alone again. Thank God for my sister and my friends who come and visit me often. They help me keep my sanity. When the kids got home at 4:30 p.m., we went to Carolyn's for supper. I enjoyed the time there.

The kids upset me though because they got in a physical fight. I was ashamed of them, because they hurt me in front of my dear friend, who was trying to help. I don't know how to deal with them, because I don't know how strict I should be on punishing them.

We came home at 8 p.m. so Carolyn could do my bandage changes. We were just about finished when Crystal answered the phone. She said it was grandpa. He talked to Crystal a few minutes and he ask for me.

The conversation went as follows:

Grandpa: How are you?

Me: Okay, physically, emotionally never.

Grandpa: How are things?

Me: It's hard (shaky voice)

The kids start their counseling tomorrow. I started my counseling last week. Went to welfare.

Grandpa: They didn't want to give you nothing did they?

Me: Very little!

Surprised Call

Grandpa: Do you want this to go to trial?

Me: That is Mark's decision.

Grandpa: Do YOU want this to go to trial?

Me: I was told that is Mark's decision.

Grandpa: It's up to you.

Me: Tell Mr. Rubenstein to call my lawyer.

Grandpa: He did, your lawyer would not talk to him.

Me: I will call my lawyer tomorrow and find out why.

Grandpa: Okay

Me: I have been told not to talk to Mr. Rubenstein. This is upsetting, I can't talk about it right now.

Grandpa: Okay

Me: Here, Crystal.

Afterward, Carolyn figured out that Grandpa was trying to get me to drop the charges, so it doesn't go to trial. My understanding is that this only goes to trial if

Mark pleads, 'not guilty'. Now I am confused again. I called my lawyer at home around 9:15 p.m. By 11:15 p.m. he still hasn't returned my call, so I go to bed.

Mark's father, like his mother in an earlier chapter, wants to talk me into dropping charges so he can get released in 6 months. This is called shock probation. Which I would not agree too.

Lawyer

January 29th, 1991

I decided to call my lawyer Mr. Whalen at home, he was not there. At 11:30 p.m. he returned my call. This is our conversation.

Me: Mark's dad called me. What is going on?

Mr. W: Why did you talk to him?

Me: I didn't, I told him I would call you. How does this work?

Mr. W: They want to plea bargain.

Me: Is it my decision?

Mr. W: No, if you refuse to testify the state can make you.

Me: You wouldn't talk to Jack Rubenstein.

Mr. W: Yes, I did, two times, I have a meeting with him on Thursday.

Me: Mark is writing me letters.

Mr. W: Call my secretary and make a sit-down appointment. Call me Thursday and ask about the meeting also.

I learned from this conversation that I am not to talk to any of Mark's family members.

Depressed

January 30th, 1991

Here I am again, sitting in the University Hospital room waiting for pharmacy supplies. My clinic visit isn't until next Wednesday, but because I ran out of Kerflex gauge, here I am. This frustrates me. This is just another problem Mark has caused me.

Keeping my memory on all of this is easy, but the war crisis helps also. As bad as the war is this helps with my problems. I was only there an hour today. I try when being depressed to put my mind on other things that is going on in the world around me. I am a believer that whatever happens to one, there is always someone else, somewhere in a lot worse shape dealing with more serious problems than me.

Counseling

January 30th, 1991

At 4:00 we all went to Northwest Mental Health Counseling Services. We have a very nice counselor. Crystal was overcome by his beard. She talked a whole lot. Seth had a very smart attitude towards him. Paul was good at handling this.

He is a very nice man and easy to talk to. I enjoy conversating with him. We talked about the incident and about how I had been handling the kids. He said, "I couldn't do any better than what I had already done." This made me feel better. He spoke to the kids alone also.

When we left at 5:30, I knew Crystal felt comfortable with him and Seth is still willing to talk to him. We will be going to counseling again next week. There are lots of answers that need to be dealt with through counseling! I am a believer in counseling as long as all people involved want to be helped. At this time, I am sure that the counseling will help me and my 8-year-old daughter. My 12-year-old son on the other hand is not a talker and does not open up to anyone except his grandmother. Only future sessions will tell.

Family Visit

January 30th, 1991

At 6:00 p.m. Mark's brother came to see us. The kids were glad to see him too. We had a very nice visit. He was really sincere with his visit. He didn't ask any questions. He let me know that Mark doesn't look good at all. He has lost a lot of weight. He agrees that Mark should be punished, but he don't know how. Even he says, "The Bible says, we reap what we sow."

He says his dad is upset and hurt. His mom is on the verge of a nervous breakdown. He's not allowed to talk about the mess. He asks me for a hug which I know he cares. I told him when this is all over, I have a lot of things to tell him.

We all have to just sit and wait till the next step begins. Before he left at 7:15 p.m. he gave me his number at work to call him if I need him. I said I would call him. Mark's brother's visit was a puzzle to me. He didn't try to convince me to make any court changes. I feel like he wanted to help, but I wasn't sure if he should.

An Officer's Concern

February 1st, 1991

Tonight around 6 p.m. Officer Angela Hunan stopped by to see us. I had spoken with her earlier on the phone and she wanted to come by and see how we were doing. Crystal was glad to see her. She was thrilled with the uniform. Crystal had pictured her as someone bad, because this person took her daddy away. Crystal asked her, "if she had handcuffed her dad?"

Officer Hunan said, "yes." She then preceded to tell Crystal that her father had cooperated with her. He did everything she asked of him. The handcuffs were only on till they got to the police station. She questioned and talked with him for an hour and a half and then she took him to the Hamilton County Justice Center.

Crystal told her, that she asked daddy, "why he didn't help me after I was burned?" Then Officer Hunan preceded to tell her that Mark did help me, because he was the one that called the life squad instead of running away. While this is true, I prefer to accept the fact that he didn't help me. He had no choice but to call the life squad. He only did that to cover his self.

Anyway, while she was here her boss, Officer Myers, radio 'ed her. She had him stop by to see us too. He was a nice man. They visited for about an hour and a half. Seth sat and ate the whole time with very little to say. (She did show up while we were eating supper together.)

We thanked them for coming and Crystal had Officer Hunan promise to come back again. I am sure the neighbors wondered why two police cars were in my driveway again. At least this time they were here on friendlier terms, not because of violence.

I was very appreciative that the officers cared enough to return and explain to my children why their father had to be arrested and taken to jail. At a later time, Officer Hunan told me that they came over because they didn't want the children thinking that officers were bad for taking their father away.

Dad's Call

February 1st, 1991

Here it is Friday night again. The children are waiting for Mark to call. He is supposed to call around 9 p.m. Crystal got upset and cried because she thought he forgot. Well, bingo at 10:45, he finally calls. I was just about to finish putting her to bed.

The general conversation for Crystal starting with, "dad you are in a new world" (his first letter). She talked about her counseling with Paul B. She told him about her uncle seeing us. She also said she is afraid to go out. She told him that Janet and Terri take her to school. She also told him that she was handling the situation good, and not crying a lot.

She asked, "dad is it fun in jail?"

He said, "not fun."

He likes to tell her he's not locked in. Maybe he isn't locked in his cell all day, but he is still locked in that justice center all day, every day, and will be for a long time until he goes to prison. He makes jail sound like an O.K.

place. He seems to enjoy telling her that he sweeps and mops the floors during third shift.

Crystal told him that Officer Hunan and Mark Myers were there. He was wondering why, I could tell. Mark told her that he talks to guards and the other inmates. He talked about how he would have to work in prison and even go to school for free to work on computers and printing.

Crystal asked him, "are you afraid to go to prison?"

He said, "I'm going to make the best of it." He also mentions that when he gets out, they will go fishing, feed the ducks, and all that stuff. (This never did take place.)

"You should always ask God to let me out," he adds. "Pray for me all the time, even in your Sunday School class. When I get out, I have 4 special people I want you to meet." The conversation continued as followed:

Crystal: Mom will be going to school for free too. Dad, you don't get to do what you want to. I get to watch television and read mostly.

Mark: Why don't you crawl through the phone holes and I'll send you back later? (Crystal thought this was funny)

Crystal: Dad, see you sometime. I miss you a lot. I love you a lot. I like your lips you put on the letter. Bye, I love you.

Dad's Call

Then Seth got on the phone and this is how their conversation went:

Mark: How are you?

Seth: O.k. I guess.

Mark: Did you like your counseling?

Seth: No, I don't.

Mark: Well, hang in there, it's to help you. What do you think of the war?

Seth: I'm too sick to talk about it. (He had a cold)

Mark: How's your comic book coming?

Seth: I'm on my 5th comic now.

Mark: How is mommy doing?

Seth: Horrible

Mark: I love you. Does this situation bother you at all?

Seth: No, I'm going to throw up.

Dark Shadows

Few moments later:

Seth: We have been watching movies. The other grades are taking achievement testing. Jobs and school in prison we saw on television.

Mark: Don't believe everything you see on television. Prison isn't all like that. They show the mean guys on television. How's mom doing?

Seth: I'm not allowed to tell you.

Mark: That's o.k. Grandma and Marvin were here today. Always write, I love you.

Seth: Dad, I liked the cat comic

Mark: That's good. I'll try to send more.

Seth: Thanks for the letter too. When are you locked up?

Mark: Only at night, I have guards to talk to.

Seth: Bye, I love you. See you sometime.

Mark: Pray for me.

Seth: Mom says when I see you depends on whether or not you plead guilty or not.

Mark: Well, we'll see.

Seth: I care about you.

Mark: I care about you too.

Seth: Bye, I love you.

Mark: I love you too.

The phone call ended at 11:25 p.m.

My feelings about this phone conversation upsets me. He tries to make Seth and Crystal feel that the jail is an o.k. place. He wants them to believe that it's fun. JAIL ISN'T FUN! Whether he is locked up at night or day he's still locked up, in the four walls, and can't get out at Main and Sycamore streets in downtown, Cincinnati. He never tells them he needs to be there! He never tells them he sent himself there! He never tells them it will be a long time before he gets out!

It looks like he is going to take this to trial to try to lessen a sentence and put off being transferred to prison. This shows me he just wants to delay seeing his kids. He only cares about what happens to Mark. Well, I fight dirty too. I will play his game of trial. I know he will be hurt in the long run, not me. He wouldn't be seeing his kids much at all. You just wait and see how he hurts when this happens, won't he hurt then?

He has to realize how much he has hurt me!
Hurt me how?
He tormented me.
He kept me in fear.
He threatened me.
He burned 20% of my body.
He has caused me a horrible amount of fear.
He has hurt me with a financial burden.
He has caused me to lose my jobs.
He has caused my family to hurt and hate.
He has caused me to be a welfare applicant.
He has caused me to file for divorce.
He has caused me to file for a civil suitcase.
He wants this to go to trial.
He has caused me to need counseling.
He has caused me to be emotionally a mess.
He has caused a change without no medical care.
He caused me to miss Christmas with my kids.
He caused us to miss Christmas with his family.
He caused New Years to come in with sadness instead of gladness.

He has hurt our church, PTA members, family friends, neighbors, so many people who thought so much of him. This I will never understand.

You know what really hurts me the most…..

Dad's Call

He hurt his kids:
They have no daddy to be with.
They have no daddy to play with.
They have no daddy to go places with.
He put a financial burden on them also.
They will have to without a lot.
They have to go to emotional counseling.
They miss him a lot.
They can't touch him when they want.
They can't kiss him goodnight.
He's not here when they are sick.
He's not here to help with homework.
He's not here to see them laugh.
He's not here to eat with them.

He's not here to help when they need dad instead of mom.

Now he's just their father who's in jail. Who I allow to call and write to them once a week? I'm not even sure if that's a good idea. For now, it comes from my heart.

Help from a Doctor

February 2nd, 1991

Today I had to deal with another frustration caused by this mess that Mark has us in. This morning I awoke to see that my son, Seth, has strep throat. I called my pediatrician of 10 years and they would not see him unless I would pay cash. They do not accept Medicaid patients. I called friends trying to find a doctor that would see Seth on this Saturday morning. I finally called my sister, Shonda, and she told me to call her friend, Gena, I did!

Gena gave me her doctors number. Just so happens that he was in his office today. I drove over there praying he would see Seth. Dr. Bowles does not take appointments on Saturdays, you take your turn once you sign in. I went in and explained the situation to him and he saw Seth right away. Another prayer answered! He didn't charge me, he just said to call in with my Medicaid number once I receive it. He gave me free cough syrup and an amoxicillin prescription.

Help from a Doctor

He wanted to give it to me in free samples too, but he was out of this medicine. I am so thankful for God's blessings and the people he puts into my life. However, I hurt Crystal today, because of the stuff going on I took my frustration out on her. I am sorry for this and told her so. She understands maturely. I am proud of her!

Back to School

February 4th, 1991

Today I sold ice cream at school again for the first time since this incident. This made me feel good. The kids were polite, the teachers showed their concern, and a lot of people were glad to see me. I did have a disturbing conversation with a worker. We talked it out. I also spoke with Mr. Myers about her and my version of what's going to happen next.

Today I also attended my first board meeting since the incident. This was o.k., except talking about the Tyler fire and Mark's membership upset me some. I am doing my best to deal with all of this.

It was good to get back to my volunteer work today. This is another way of therapy for me. I need a lot more of this. I am limited to when I go though because of these bandage changes. I need to work on this!

A New Nurse

February 4th, 1991

Today Shonda had to go to work at 10 p.m. This meant that she could no longer do my nighttime bandage change. I have to find someone else! I have a board meeting to attend at 7:30, which means it will be too late for Carolyn to come down to do it. I decide to call my friend Teri, she agrees to do it.

I got home at 9:45 and Teri came at 10:15. I made us some coffee. We finished watching a movie. At 11:15 or so we did my bandage change. Teri did a good job, except she made me laugh. She was afraid to touch me. She thought the burns were really bad. I could see in her face doing this for me was like hurting herself. The concern in her eyes was really sincere. She cares about me a whole lot. She is very special to me and such a good friend. Having my friends and my family to come daily is a lot to ask. I love and appreciate all of them because they take the time to come and change my burn bandages.

Busy Day

February 5th, 1991

Today started as a normal school morning. Seth missed his bus. I drove him to school 10 minutes late. My best friend Carolyn came to visit at 9:15. I was glad she did. We sat and drank coffee and talked. I had two good cries with her. I find myself crying with her more than anyone else. She is also very special to me. While she was here, she did my bandage change.

I decided to do a lot of cleaning today. Wouldn't you know, my bandages were falling off by 5 p.m., because of all the movement. Also, this frustrates me because, no matter what I do we can't keep these bandages tight.

I had to go get Seth at 1:30 from school. I think it's his nerves. He doesn't say much at all. I worry about him. Shonda came over at 9 p.m. to do the bandages. We had a slight argument. I believe we are getting on each other's nerves. I need to be a lot more polite to her. I will work on this.

Busy Day

Seth as a sixth grader in middle school has a lot to deal with. He feels embarrassed for his friends to know what his father did to his mother. I hurt for him, but outside of counseling I can't do much to help him. I wish I could take all his emotional pain away. Only God can do this. I pray for my children every day, and trust that they too are praying to God for help.

Medical Blessing

February 6th, 1991

Today all in all has been a day of blessings. My mother and my aunt came up to spend the day. We all had a good visit. Shonda came over at 11:30 a.m. At 12:15 we left for clinic. I went in at 1 p.m. sharp. The good news is that there will be no skin grafting done. The lower arm and upper shoulder can be left uncovered. I go back next week to see when I have to wear the Jobst vest. (A jobst vest is a very tight spandex compression vest to help flatten the burns when scarring. I had to wear this for 9 months.)

At 2 p.m. we went to the pharmacy and sit till 3:20 p.m. waiting for my prescriptions. This is such a long and frustrating ordeal. Time is of no importance to them at all.

We got home at 4:15 p.m. We picked up the kids. Mom went home with Shonda for supper. My aunt Cindy had supper with me. She left around 6 p.m. I enjoyed her visit though. She means a lot to me. At 7 p.m. we went to Shonda's to ride to church in the van. Church starts at 7:30 p.m.

Everett Kinney (a good friend of mine) told me that Mark called him this morning. He told Everett that he wrote a letter to the church again. Our pastor, did not read it! Everett said that Mark seems upset, concerned, and sorry finally. He also told Everett that he didn't want this to go to trial. This is hard for me to believe. Mark also told Everett that on February 13th, him and I, and our lawyers are supposed to have a meeting together. (I guess I will hear about this tomorrow when I see Mr. Whalen.) I know I can't sit in a room with him under any circumstances!

Well, this remains to be seen! I have so many feelings about all of this. All mixed feelings too. Right now, my kids are sick. Seth told me that he hurts in his heart and is very unhappy. I still cannot help him here. All I can do is give them both lots of love and extra attention, with a lot of concern touched by lots of hugs and prayers.

Cards

February 6th, 1991

Today I received a card from Mark. Following:
Thoughts of you (front)

Inside:

We are far apart,
Yet within my thoughts
I share each day
I am thinking of you

This card does not make me sympathize with him at all. In a way it's kinda funny. In another way it's scary. There has to be something wrong with his way of thinking. He also wrote in the card to the kids the following:

You both have the best mom in the world. Please love her and help her, and pray for her each day. Say hi to mommy and tell her that I love her and miss her as well.

How can he say he loves me after doing this to me? He is very emotionally sick. I could never love him again! Not ever! Right now, I don't love him at all!

Crystal and Seth received Valentine's Day cards from Mark's aunt Lyda and uncle Clyde today. This shows me that they do care about the kids. I would like for her to call Crystal soon.

I received a sympathy card from Lyda today. This has really touched me. She says, the following:

Come down (Corbin, Kentucky.) if you think you can ever make it. I'm sorry about the tragedy. I'm sorry about what has happened. Hope he gets what he deserves. What he did, no use in him doing that, I'm talking about my nephew. I think he could have done something instead of burning you.

Love you, Lyda and Clyde

This card tells me that Lyda still loves me, that she wants to see me, and she believes that he should be punished. I knew Lyda would care about me, with or without, Mark at my side. I love deeply and divorced or not I always will love and care about her.

Mr. Whalen's (my lawyer) Visit

February 7th, 1991

Here is what Mark wants:
His dad tried to scare me into thinking that I shouldn't want this to go to trial. Honestly, Mark is the one who doesn't want this to go to trial. Mark wants me to plea bargain on a lesser prison sentence such as 7 to 10 years instead of 10 to 15 years.

I will not do this. I am willing to wait and see how far he will take this. He should know if this goes to trial, he is only hurting himself. The jury trial will find him guilty and will add more years on top of his sentencing.

Mom paid the divorce filing fee so that Mark could see in print that I am divorcing him. She also gave Mr. Whalen a love offering. We all honestly believe that Mark thinks I will let him come back to me. I was so glad Mr. Whalen answered a lot of her questions. She did finally accept a lot of his answers too! Filing for the divorce is the 1st step for me in realizing that Mark can never be a part of my life again. I'm moving forward. (Praise God)

Back to Work

February 8th, 1991

Today I decided to clean a house for Kathy. I need the money to get Seth some new gym shoes for Track and Field. I started at 10:30 and I finished at 1:30. I took a half-hour lunch break. I am frustrated over this time limit. It shows me that my burns and tiredness slow me down a whole lot.

There is so much going through my mind concerning working. So many decisions to make about this. I don't know whether to keep on working or to get a real job, which I know I have to do later on anyway. By a real job I mean for a company or business where I am always getting a weekly paycheck. Cleaning private homes is okay, but only one week brings in just $30. That's not enough to support my children and myself.

Dad Calls Again

February 8th, 1991

Seth answered the phone. He told Mark "That he hated his guts" and "that he was a bad person."

Mark: No, I'm not read 1John 1:9, there is a lot of good people here.

Seth: They're not good people, they're in jail.

Mark: That's beside the point

Crystal: Hi, daddy!

Mark: Crystal, you don't hate me, do you?

Crystal: Did you get the comic I sent? And the letter- love in my heart?

Mark: Don't you ever change your feeling for daddy.

Dad Calls Again

Crystal: No, you hurt mommy! You bad daddy, bad. You're a bad boy!

Mark: I want you to meet some people someday.

Crystal: Who?

Mark: Floyd Hyatt, Gretchen, Joy, and Laura

Crystal: We are going to Michelle Tanners wedding. I wish you could go.

Mark: Okay.

Crystal: Dad, tell grandma Gibbs I need money for new shoes.

Mark: Sounds like mommy and Seth are upset.

Crystal: Well, I'm not too much upset.

Seth: Daddy, mommy is always upset.

Mark: I have to go now. Someone else wants to use the phone.

Seth: Okay, here's Crystal. Bye dad, I love you.

Mark: I love you too.

Crystal: Dad, moms met a guy called Art. (Crystal didn't say this right. I wanted her to say, "was going to meet a guy named Art. Well, let Mark think a guy is seeing me.)

Mark: Sounds like she's getting happy.

Seth: Dad it's true.

Mark: Tell her to keep her lip stuck up. (We all laughed about this.)

Seth: Bye dad.

Mark: I've got to go.

Crystal: Bye dad, I love you.

Mark: Ask mom if I can call on Saturday? To have more time to talk.

I said "No", only if we aren't home on Friday night.

Mark: Okay

Crystal: Bye, I love you and miss you.

Mark: I love you too.

You can read that through these phone calls my children are so confused. It's going to take a lot of time for them to deal with all of this in a way that helps except what has happened to us as a family.

Marvin and Kids Visit

February 9th, 1991

Last night Mark's brother, called me and ask to bring his kids to come and see us on Saturday. I told him around noon would be fine. They came at 12:30. The kids were really glad to see me. They all played fairly well. Of course, Crystal's room looked like a cyclone hit it. Marvin bought White Castle for us all to eat.

Marvin and I talked about me, Mark, feelings, him, Joanie (his wife), and things of the past., the kids, prison, and other things. He explained to me what to expect if I take the kids to see Mark. I was surprised to learn that he is not in the justice center. He is in the jail above the courthouse. This explains why we have been sending mail to the Hamilton County Jail.

Marvin says, "Take the elevator to the 5th floor. Walk up the steps and a guard will let you in the 6th floor. The gates shut behind you, then they take you to a visitor's room. You talk with a phone and see through a glass window. Marvin says Mark's eyes are all bloodshot. No

Marvin and Kids Visit

white in them at all. He doesn't sleep much at all. He has lost weight. He is nervous. When he calls the kids it's a front to act like everything is okay. He mops the floor on 3rd shift.

Marvin sends him pens, paper, and stamps through the mail. All of his mail is searched. You can't take anything to him at all. Everything is screened. Marvin also told me that Mark will break when he sees the kids. This will cause him to wish he was out. Mark never talks about me. He still shows no remorse whatsoever. He scares me even though he is in prison.

Marvin says, "their dad has still not been to see Mark!" He doesn't know why! Also, his mother doesn't go every Friday either. She is an emotional mess. I feel sorry for her. I still pray for her. I am allowed to take the kids to see them though. Now, (Mark's sister) she is still blaming me. Marvin proceeds to tell me how Mark feels or looks in jail. I really don't care. He put himself there. Even being a Christian, it's hard for me to have any sympathy for him. Why should I? He's the criminal, I'm the victim, along with his children.

Big Night Out (The Wedding)

February 9th, 1991

At 7 o'clock the kids and I went to Michelle went to my friend's wedding. The wedding was at Niagara St. Baptist Church. The reception was at a party hall in Mt. Healthy. We went in at 7:50 p.m. and sit down. When Carolyn came in, we sit with their friends from West Virginia. We knew no one, they knew no one. We had a nice time talking. We enjoyed watching everyone dance. I enjoyed watching Crystal learn to dance. She really had a good time. This would have sure made Mark mad.

I sit and talk with Carolyn's friend from West Virginia, a lady named Sandy. Her 13- and 15-year-old daughter taught Crystal how to dance. We left the reception hall at 12:30 a.m. We were all very exhausted too. Crystal and I went to bed at 2 a.m. Seth stayed up watching television till 4 a.m. We all slept well! This was our first real night out after the tragedy. We all had a good time. It was great to not think about all the bad, and just enjoy other people and see some true happiness.

Outside Jail Tour

February 11th, 1991

At 5 p.m. today, February 11th, 1991, Carolyn drove Crystal and I downtown to the courthouse building. She needed to know where Mark was at. We drove to one side and stopped. I explained the rows of barred windows to her. Told her that daddy was above the barred windows where the little, tiny windows were.

Then we drove in front of the main steps. I told her that we go up the steps inside, into an elevator, up more steps to see her dad. I told her that he cannot go outside of that building. He can't go down past the 5th floor either. Then I showed her the tunnel where he is transported from jail to the courtrooms.

Now maybe, at least she knows where he is at. She would not let me take her into the building though. She didn't want to go in at all! She still doesn't want to see Mark. Now we will wait and see if this relieves some the missing part.

This trip was suggested by the counselor to ease Crystal's mind of why her dad was not coming back home. I think she has excepted where he will be for a long time now.

Valentine's Day Cards

February 11th, 1991

The following is a letter Seth sent to Mark for Valentine's Day:

Dear dad,

I am sending this comic book as a Valentine's present. You will get one whenever. The one I am sending you is No.1. Dad, Crystal, mom, and Carolyn went downtown. Crystal will tell you why they went downtown when you call on Friday.

We are doing good here at home. Mom gets upset because just about every day a new problem is there she has to face, because of you. Me and Crystal are doing good in counseling. Crystal misses you a lot. I am doing pretty good except when there is a problem. I don't like and get very mad at you. Even sometimes I take my anger out on mom and Crystal.

Dad, I have been writing to Brad's (Seth's friend) uncle. Mom has a pen pal over there. Mom doesn't know how often they can write. If I have more information, I will tell you Friday when you call. Dad, I love you and I miss the things we used to do together, but we can't because of you. I hope to see you soon. I am not really sure when I can see you, but I can bet that it will be after the mess. Well, goodbye

Love,
Seth Gibbs

Crystal sent Mark a Valentine's Day card. She put lipstick on her lips and kissed the card to send him a kiss. She sent a little kids Valentine's Day card too. Also, a picture that she colored. Of course, she said, "I love you and miss you." No matter what her dad would have done, Crystal, will always love him. I am okay with this except Mark shows no intention of really explaining to our children how serious of a crime he has committed.

Bad News Day

February 13th, 1991

Today I had one bad news after another. At 11 a.m. Jerry Krumlebeck (prosecuting attorney) called. Him, Jack Reubenstein, and Judge Ann Marie Tracy had a pre-trial. The prosecutor agreed to let Jack Reubenstein plead to felonious assault. Tracy could give him 3-8-15 years. She gave him till March 12th to make a final decision. Then he has 30 days to either set a trial date or be sentenced. Looks like he will be in the Hamilton County jail till at least the end of April.

This goes to show you that our Ohio justice system is more for the criminal than the victim. I am very angry with this! Nothing is going my way and to linger on until Mark is to be sentenced. I guess I need to pray more and put this sentencing in the Lord's hands. You reap what you sow and you pay the consequences. Maybe, in some time I will figure out how and why it is this way. For now, I just wonder and think.

Second of all today at the clinic the therapist (Beth), puts a temporary burn vest on me. It's very hard to get on and off by myself. Mine has not been made yet until my Medicaid card has been approved. The burn vest is needed because my neck and my arm needs tightness now. I already feel like it is choking me. It's going to take a lot of getting used to. At least the permanent one will have breast cups. Right now, this temporary one is squeezing my breast together.

It's ironic, but the two things Mark knew I feared the most was fire and choking. He burnt me and choked me in August and now I have to wear a tight neck support which is also choking me. Wearing a skin tight burns jobst vest is so uncomfortable, but I know it is needed to keep the scars down and not look so bumpy on my neck and arms. He still has the best of me. Well, I'll pray about this. I guess in some ways, he is dealing also with being closed in, not getting to listen to his precious tapes. That is punishment itself.

Valentine's Day Apart

February 14th, 1991

This is a very unusual day. My feelings should be love and closeness to Mark. Instead, I am going downtown to sign divorce papers. This is so hard for me to do. This is a feared, forced, divorce, but what can I do? I could never live with him again. I will always be afraid of him because of this violent crime.

I took Crystal to school and then I picked up Teri (my friend). We went downtown to my counseling session. These sessions make me feel angry. I mean, I get anger out. Myra (advocate for women helping women) is glad to see me angry. I need some anger. The longer I wait for Mark's sentencing the angrier I get. Sometime soon I plan to let some or all of this anger out on Mark, we'll see!

Woman Helping Women is a free service that helps women in abusive relationship.

At 11:15 a.m. Teri and I went into the courthouse. We got on the elevator and went up to the 5th floor. We asked for the jail entrance. We went through the door and up the steps. We were surprised by what we saw. We stepped into the visitors' room and to the right of me was little phone booths. This is where visitors could talk to prisoners with phones and through glass. On the left was a barred cage looking door. Standing inside the door was a jail guard.

I told him I was Mark G's wife. I asked him, "Is Mark allowed to receive presents?" He said, "no, only 6 pair of underwear, 6 pairs of socks, 6 t-shirts." Well, this is things Thelma bought and took to him. He said, "Mark's mail is all screened, but Seth's comic books can go by." Books are not permitted either. He asked me 3 times if I wanted to see Mark. I said, "no, I'm not allowed." Finally, when he asked me the 3rd time, I asked him if he was married? He said, "yes." Then I asked him, "If you torched your wife, would she visit you?" He said, "no." we said our goodbyes. At least now I know how to prepare the kids when they decide to go see him.

Next, we went over to Mr. Whalen's office. I signed four divorce papers. These papers weren't even typed up yet. I didn't even read what I was signing. This was silly of me. I didn't have time anyway. I gave the secretary a $200 check, then we left.

Teri and I went to Frisch's for lunch. While we were here, she handed me an envelope. I put it in my purse. It was nice to have her treat me out to lunch. We enjoyed this time together. At 1:00 p.m. we came to the house. She come to help me get my Jobst vest on. I took the envelope and opened it. Inside was a lovely note and $100 from

Valentine's Day Apart

her and Bill. (I still have this in a safety deposit box as an emergency keepsake.) I cried a lot. Tears of happiness, of course. She cares about us so very much. She is so special. (Another blessing from the Lord.)

The Lord daily sends me a special blessing someone either gives me a word of praise, a card sent, money or some item dropped off. People really do care. It's nice to be so loved by friends and acquaintances. At 2:00 p.m. I went to Crystal's Valentine's party. I enjoyed seeing all the kids and also talking to Miss Faye (Crystal's teacher). She is such a blessing as my friend and also as Crystal's teacher. I showed Faye my lower arm burn. She was shocked at how it looked. She hurts for me so much too. We got home at 3:30 p.m.

At 4 p.m. I took the kids to their counseling session with Paul. Crystal seems to enjoy this; Seth is still carrying a chip on his shoulder. Paul always gives me words of encouragement. He is well pleased with how I handle the problems the kids deal with. It's hard to say how long the kids will have to go see him, and it's hard to say when they are exactly being helped. The need is there, but the how to solve is very difficult to handle. This is another matter of deep prayer for answers.

At 5 p.m. we stopped at a friend's house. I felt I owed them an explanation of maybe why this happened to me. They are very caring, and praying for us. We got home at 6:30 p.m. Around 7 p.m. two of Mark's family showed up. I broke down in tears. I thought he came to see the kids, but he didn't, he came to plead for me to drop the charges. Which I have been told I cannot drop. I have decided that either Jack Ruebenstein or Jerry is lying to one of us. Elzie must believe that I can lessen Mark's sentence time in prison. Well, I guess this remains to be seen, but someone misunderstands! I am determined to fight to find out who is telling the truth.

Some of the conversation:

Elzie: Talked about money he is spending for Mark's lawyer.

Me: I told him that his taxes also pay for the state to prosecute Mark too.

Elzie: Tried to guarantee me that Mark would never hurt me again.

Me: I told him to buy me a house in Timbuktu and give me 3 plane tickets and never let Mark cross the border, then I would let Mark out. (My anger speaking)

Elzie: He said Mark would never take my children. It's against the law.

Me: I told him Mark always threatened to take them and divorced fathers break the law all the time.

Elzie: He told me he knew Mark wouldn't.

Me: I told him Mark always kept Seth in fear.

Seth: Told grandpa about the time on Easter Sunday when Mark grabbed the steering wheel and almost made us wreck.

Me: I told him that if this goes to trial there is a lot more to come out to.

A lot was said, some anger, some concern, and some upsetting words. Elzie left here crying, and I was very upset. Marvin came because he had no choice. He was hurting for me and crying, I could tell he wanted nothing to do with this. They left at 9:15 p.m. I told Marvin to wait till I called Carolyn. She came down and I cried so hard while we talked.

Depressed for Sure

February 15th, 1991

Today was such a bad day! Elzie being here last night hurt me a lot. Today I decided to volunteer at PRMS for the pizza party and the dance. I was at school from 1:00-5:30 p.m. I couldn't wait to leave. It just wasn't like before. I guess this mess interfered with the enjoyment. I used to have fun with school volunteer work.

Carolyn kept Crystal so I went back to her house. We had some coffee and talked, we all decided to go to Frisch's, then we went to Carolyn's daughter's apartment. I let Crystal decide whether we should go because she might miss Mark's phone call. She said she didn't care. Well, we got home 15 minutes before Mark called. Boy, was she glad!

Well, we had a nice day except for I stayed depressed. Crystal and I didn't want to come home, but we had to. Sometimes though, it is very hard on all of us. We'll have to pray that this becomes easier as each day comes.

Mark's Call

February 15th, 1991

Mark assured Crystal that he only had 30 minutes exact tonight. They talked about Carolyn, Michelle, bed, sleep, George and Russell's game, the wedding, dancing, counseling, and visitors. Also, I told Mark not to talk about me any more (hollering through the phone so he could hear me). Seth talked about his comic books, about Marvin crying, grandpa pleading, and how he upset all of us. He told Mark it was hard to talk and didn't want to talk anymore. Crystal back on the phone, not much to say, no talking, mostly yawning.

Crystal: I don't learn memory verses.

Mark: I learn a lot of memory verses.

Crystal: Valentine card!

Mark: It's real cold.

Crystal: Ice on Carolyn's driveway. Our house is warm and cold. Is it cold down there?

Mark: It's real warm here.

Crystal: Dad, money is getting low. Phone calls are expensive!

Mark: 4 Friday's is 2.80!

Tonight, I took the phone from Crystal and I said the following:

Me: Mark, did you ask your dad to come up here and plead for you?

Mark: NO!

Me: I have a lot to say to you, I'm not allowed to yet! Make this easier on us and get this over with.

(Then, I paused to allow him to tell me he was sorry, but of course he didn't.) I gave Crystal the phone back while I cried and hit the wall.

Crystal: Dad I'm going to hang up now. Bye, dad. I love you!

Mark: Bye now.

Mark's Call

I made a few phone calls myself. I called Teri and talked with her for a few minutes. Then I called Elzie! I told him I gave Mark the chance to tell me he was sorry, but he didn't. His response was, "I'm tired of talking, I'm washing my hands of the whole thing." He said he helped Mark and I and that I won't do anything for him. Then, he said it was J.R.'s idea for him to come see me.

I believe that Thelma had a lot to do with Elzie coming up though. After all, Elzie told me that not even his son is worth $200. Even if he had the money, he wouldn't bail him out. This proves that Thelma made him come and plead to me. Well, I hurt for them and I pray for them daily. Mark has messed up their lives along with mine and the kids. He is so mixed up. Some day he will have to answer for all this pain he has caused on so many people.

Pictures

February 16th, 1991

I went through picture's today. I gave the kids the last 5x7 picture of Mark and I which was taken on our 14th anniversary. I told them that this picture is the last one together of me and their dad they will ever have.

A couple hours later Crystal told me that she wanted the family picture put in her room. I immediately took it down and hung it in her room. I told her later I will go get us a new family picture without Mark. We are a family of 3 now, not 4!

Seth lashed out at me with a lot of anger tonight. I just listened. This anger was a different kind of anger. This outburst proves that he is missing Mark! I cried and went to Teri's. there we had a good laugh together. I went there so she could help me put my best on. I then talked to Carolyn on the phone, I needed this time.

February 17th, 1991

At about 1:30 a.m. I called aunt Cindy, and got her out of bed. I needed a good cry and a good close relative to

Pictures

talk to. She understands me a lot. She seems to help me a lot too because we are so close. She is also so special to me. We talked until 3 a.m. (my phone bill is going to be high). I needed this call though. I just won't make a habit of this though. We all slept in late and we didn't go to church because of Crystal's strep throat.

I went through and sorted more pictures today. I put pictures of the kids from newborn till now in a box for Mark. I finally had to quit because I started to get upset and began to shake. Looking at those pictures is hard to do. There are so many memories there. Good times and bad times. I will decide what to do with all of these later.

Guess Who Called?

February 19th, 1991

At 10 a.m. the phone rang. I was shocked, to my surprise, it was Mark! He got an inmate to call on his phone and his wife transferred the call to me by a 3-way phone. This way I was not charged for the call. At first, I paused for a few minutes. Then, he asked, "Are you there?" I said, "What do you want?"

Mark: I apologize for what I did.

(I didn't accept this as an apology because he still hasn't said he's sorry)

Mark: Will you agree to me being sentenced for two years?

Me: Mark, I am turning that decision over to Judge Tracy and the Lord.

Mark: Okay, I will accept that.

Me: Will you make your decision and get it over with? Quit drawing this out. If you care about me and the kids you will sign everything, I want over to me.

Mark: What do you want?

Me: Car, house, life insurance

Mark: I need a car.

Me: Your dad will get you another car. I need the money for the kids.

Mark: You can't afford the house?

Me: I don't know, but at least if it's in my name I have more of an option to work this out. You know Seth doesn't want to leave this house.

Mark: I'll think about it.

Me: If you care about me and you love your kids you will sign what I ask.

Mark: I do care!

Me: Do you want me to file bankruptcy?

Mark: No.

Me: Then do what I ask to make this easier on all of us. Make your plead now, you already know you don't want this to go to trial.

Mark: The state doesn't want to put the money out either.

Me: Your dad doesn't want to put more money on Jack Rubenstein either. Why didn't you just leave? If you hated me so much, why didn't you just move out? You didn't have to burn me.

Mark: I don't know, I should of, but you were going to leave me in March.

Me: I was going to leave that up to you. I didn't want it this way. Why didn't you leave normally so the kids could see you with regular visitation rights like a father is supposed to have?

Mark: I don't know.

Me: Well, I guess you will have to pay the consequences.

Mark: Tell Crystal I apologize. The phone booths are little. How is she?

Me: She is very confused. Seth is so angry I don't even know who he is anymore. He is very different.

Mark: He has a right to be.

Me: Mark, I don't have to let you call them. I don't have to mail their letters to you, and I don't have to let them read your mail, but I do!

Mark: I appreciate that! You know the pastor has not been to see me.

Me: I know, after all, you are not a member anymore. He is not your pastor. I know what he's going through. He has tears over this, because something like this happened to a family in his church.

Mark: I am glad something happened to get him to cry.

Me: Shouldn't have been this.

Mark: Can I call you again?

Me: I'm not supposed to talk to you.

Mark: This conversation is between us, you tell the prosecutor if you want to, but I'm not telling Jack (lawyer). You will be getting a letter from me tomorrow, you can read it or throw it away, or let the prosecutor read it. I don't care.

Me: The next time you call me, I want to hear your decision from you, no one else. So don't call me anymore. The sooner you decide, the sooner you will see the kids.

Mark: Okay I will call Jack (lawyer). I will think about what you want, then I will let you know. I have to hang up now. I'll call you again.

Me: Mark, I am really upset. I have to worry, wonder, and go through so much because of all this. Don't you realize you could have burnt the kids up and the house.

Mark: Yes, I do.

Me: Didn't you care at all?

Mark: I didn't think about that at the time.

Me: Just remember, I have always loved you, I always will love you, and all I ever asked in return was for you to LOVE ME BACK.

Mark: I know that. I really have to hang up.

Me: I will talk to you again when this is all over. You can call the kids on Friday.

Mark: Bye, thanks for talking to me.

Me; Bye. (I was crying really hard.)

This phone call has upset me today! I was an emotional mess all day. I couldn't even attend the PTA meeting tonight. Of course, Debbie understood. I didn't though. I hate to have a job and not carry out the responsibility of it. I don't know if this phone call from him was sincere, or to play on my sympathy, or a ploy to tell the judge that I spoke to him. I do know, Jerry K, is going to be mad, because he talked to me, and I to him. I needed to talk to him though. I needed to tell him the ways I feel. He has to know this is not okay with me. I have a lot more to say to him too. Next time will be in person though.

Even though he didn't say he was sorry, I still pray that this phone call was sincere, and he did call because he cares about us. I guess I'll find out later. I can't help but think that was a sincere phone call. The 3-way line bothers me though. This does not seem possible at all. Anyway, this phone call upset me. I proved to myself that I still have feelings for him. Most of me still loves him. A big part of me will always fear him. He is still their daddy. I want them to be in close contact with him, but these things will have to be done my way.

Even though this phone call upset me, I still went to school to sell ice cream. I told Faye about the phone call. She told me I probably did the right thing by talking to him. When I got home at 1 p.m. Teri came over to be with me. We cried together. We tried to make buttons together, we couldn't! She took them home for her and Bill to work on them. She is great to help me, I am lucky to have her for a friend. She is a friend I never want to lose.

The Truth

February 19th, 1991

I was so upset so Carolyn came down to see me. We talked about Mark's phone call. She is such a good support to me. She is another friend I never want to lose. Good friends are so hard to come by. She is special in her own way too. I need her support.

At around 8 a.m. Jerry K. called me. Finally! I called him back and the truth now comes clear to me.

Me: Why was Mark's dad up here trying to get me to drop charges? You told me I couldn't drop charges.

Jerry: That's right, you can't.

Me: How come Mark's dad thinks I can?

Jerry: They want you to tell Judge Tracy that you will agree to two years.

Me: I don't have to, do I?

Jerry: No, you will write up a victim impact statement. This will be read to me, Mark, and the lawyers. Then, Judge Tracy will ask you to recommend a sentence. You don't have to, just tell her that you are leaving that up to me.

Me: Good, I don't want my kids to say to me, "Mommy, because you told the judge 5 years, now daddy is going to do 10 years."

Jerry: Thank you, that's my job.

Me: What are you going to recommend?

Jerry: 5 years

Me: That's okay with me.

Jerry: Why did you let his dad in?

Me: I thought he was only here to see the kids.

Jerry: That's how he started, but then he changed the situation?

Me: Right, also I talked to Mark today.

Jerry: I told you not to.

Me: I needed to. We didn't talk about the case. I told Mr. Whalen I wanted to ask him to sign things over to me when I got a chance.

Jerry: You let Mr. Whalen handle all the legal stuff. Don't talk to him anymore. He wants J.R. to get in court and say, "She's been talking to him." Judge Tracy will use this against our case. Please don't talk to him or his dad anymore.

Me: Okay, I promise, I won't!

Jerry: You have to be at the sentencing, because you are the victim.

Me: Okay, I want to be there.

Jerry: I will call you for a sit-down meeting before March 12th. Jack R. wants to talk to you. If he calls, don't talk to him.

Me: Okay, Mark said he would decide his plead sooner.

Jerry: Jack R. will not let him plead before March 12th. He is doing his job. He wants to give this time to play on your sympathy.

Me: Well, it won't work, because I'm going to let you handle this your way, not mine.

Jerry: Good, I have to go now, I'll call you later for an appointment.

Me: Okay, keep me in touch with what's going on. Bye!

Jerry: Okay, bye!

Verbal Attack

February 21st, 1991

Today has all in all been a really bad day. Mom and I have had some heated arguments. The discussions are not very positive at all. Mom is so set in her mind towards things. I try to be somewhat positive and have faith that I need.

She feels that I'm not facing the reality of things. I know that I am, but I have to have enough faith to at least try to stay in my home and keep my family happy. I realize this will be hard to accomplish, but before I give up, I have to at least give it a try. As soon as Mark is sentenced and in prison, I will start looking for a job. I know this will not be easy, but I have to at least try. If I find that I can't make it, then I will move.

Seth came home and threw a fit about going to counseling. Diane talked to him. He got in the car very upset and made verbal attacks, screamed at me, cried, cursed, and beat on the car the whole way. This hurt me very much but once again I had to take it.

When we got there, he embarrassed me in front of a waiting room full of people. Paul only saw him for about 5 minutes. Seth just doesn't talk at all. He keeps a chip on his shoulder and stays very rebellious towards us about this. Well, Paul decided we would let him skip next week. I will tell him on Tuesday of next week though. Crystal enjoys talking to Paul, she talks about everything.

I need the encouragement Paul gives me. He always says things that shows me that I am doing the best I can do. I need all the encouragement that I can to get through all of this.

Mark Calls Again!

February 22nd, 1991

Mark calls again. Not much to say.

- My mother typed a letter on Monday
- Apples and oranges
- Stamps soaked apart (flower)
- Multiplication
- Comics to send!
- Pepper

Mark:

- Warm today

- Taco's

- Out to play

- Papa Gibbs

- Long letter that he wrote

Me: Seth wants to come and see you. (Pause)

Mark: What else is new?

Crystal: Dad's aren't perfect.

Mark: We all make mistakes.

Crystal: Papa Gibbs made me laugh about Ginger. (dog)

Mark: Next time, send a picture to put on the wall, bunch of cards, and comics. Actually, you keep the comics.

Crystal: Do I keep them? It's noisy.

Mark: Different guys.

Crystal: How many?

Mark: 300

Mark Calls Again!

Crystal: Do they care if you count them?

Mark: No. This phone, talk longer.

Crystal: Other people!

Mark: you asleep, I am awake.

Crystal: Late up, with no school. No school today. Conference Seth next week.

Mark: Play basketball today, 1 ½ ping pong.

Crystal: Golf, bubby talk.

Mark: Okay.

Seth: Hi dad, I don't want to talk.

Mark: Crystal, we can talk more.

Crystal: I'll always talk on Fridays.

Mark: Don't quit missing me.

Crystal: I won't. Bro. Kinney, snacks.

Mark: I talked to him last week. Church, song, people.

Crystal: Amazing! Have everything down there? Weights?

Mark: I lift weights, watch movies.

Crystal: You said that in your letter.

Mark: I am the only one up all night. Sleep whenever I want.

Crystal: Wish I could.

Mark: Next letter, something special.

Crystal: Why friends?

Mark: We aren't enemies, right?

Crystal: I guess till then.

Mark: You will like it. Too many letters, president like!

Crystal: Where do you put them?

Mark: It's hard to tell you. Stacked up.

Crystal: Seth's comic, letters?

Mark: Wilson, someone I don't know.

Mark Calls Again!

Crystal: Didn't call Dave!

Mark: I called Dave.

Crystal: Pictures in my album. Yawning, not tired.

Mark: I'll sleep tonight.

Crystal: Grandma went home. You should go to Florence. Bubble gum machine.

Mark: Yea, I've been there.

Crystal: Gum color all over me.

Mark: Pretty and sweet.

Crystal: In your stomach with you.

Mark: Wish, hug.

Crystal: Can't hug when visit.

Mark: Telephone.

Crystal: I got mommy's hugs.

Mark: Even apart, always with you. First thing, swing at park.

Crystal: Story of swing, Ernest!

Mark: Okay I remember. One of these days, back together.

Crystal: Need a lot of hugs and kisses from me. How many days?

Mark: 60 days, a lot, like 2 months.

Crystal: 6 days add 0 to make 60.

Mark: Glad I get to call.

Crystal: Yawn, you don't.

Mark: Sometimes. What else can we talk about?

Crystal: Phone sweats on my ear.

Mark: Sticks to my ear.

Crystal: Gross, sticky! Everett, ice cream.

Mark: Go get me one.

Mark Calls Again!

Crystal: Junk food

Mark: Chips, fruit, candy bars.

Crystal: Seth eats oranges.

Mark: Lots of oranges.

Crystal: How many do you eat?

Mark: 3 or 4, lots of fruit, vegetables, fish, chicken, no pizza.

Seth: War

Mark: War

Seth: Crystal back on.

Mark: What time? An hour already! Saturday- 2 hours.

Crystal: Only on Fridays.

Mark: Tired of talking?

Crystal: No.

Mark: Being quiet instead? I love you.

Crystal: I love you.

Mark: You are special to me.

Crystal: Yep, I miss you.

Mark: Yea, you, okay?

Crystal: Two good things. (Love, miss)

Mark: A guy, card, giant, bigger than you.

Crystal: Pepper, still on there.

Mark: A guy by the phone.

Crystal: Guys are loud. All I got to say, Seth talk.

Seth: Sighing

Mark: What's up?

Seth: Want to say bye?

Mark: Hang in there, I love you.

Seth: Okay.

Mark Calls Again!

Mark: Take care.

Seth: I love you, bye.

Crystal: Dad, I'll hang up now.

Mark: Okay, I love you.

Crystal: I love you.

Mark: I miss you.

Crystal: I miss you.

Mark: Talk to you next time.

Crystal: Bye.

LIAR

February, 26th, 1991

Today, Mr. Whalen called me. He told me that tomorrow he is going to serve Mark with divorce papers. Then, Mark has 28 days to sign. If he doesn't then we go to divorce court. He told me that J.R. told him that Mark had spoken to me. He said that Mark said that I didn't want a divorce. I told Mr. Whalen that this was a lie. We only talked about the kids and I wanted him to sign the house over to me. He said he would think about it.

I now know that the letters that I received from Mark on February, 2nd, and 23rd are just a bunch of butter her up lies. I thought he was very sincere and caring about me and the kids. I should have listened to Juanita, after all she said Mark will always be Mark. I guess if I was facing 2-3 years in prison then I would write fake sincere letters too. Well, this news today has hurt me, but I should have expected this in the first place.

First Request

February 27th, 1991

Marvin (Mark's brother) called and asked if he could come and see us. I said yes, as long as he didn't tell Mark he was here. He asked me if Mark could have his old glasses. I said, NO! A few minutes later he called back and wanted to know if he could bring Joanie (his girl), I said, yes.

He showed up at 7:00 p.m. Joanie wouldn't come in because she is allergic to cats. He came in with a bag of groceries. The bag had spaghetti, sauce, peanut butter, jelly, crackers, bread, cookies, and potato chips. All these except the bread came from Batavia, IL. I would like to know which store all of these came from. I will ask Marvin later. While Marvin was here, I told him to tell Mark that he can't have anything from this house until he signs the divorce papers.

The next day....

This morning my feelings are very depressing. I could of went bowling with Carolyn. I could of went to school for a retirement celebration. I could of went to school to help with Rif. Instead, I chose to stay home and be depressed this morning.

Yesterday, after Marvin left, the rest of the day nothing went right, except for Teri's birthday breakfast. I went to the clinic at 1:30 p.m. I got my Jobst vest to wear. I can't stand it! The neck is too high, the seam rubs the burn on my neck. The bend in the elbow creases and hurts. It rubs on the back elbow bone. It rubs on the left under my arm.

I was in the pharmacy till 3:40 p.m. I had to cancel Crystal's counseling session. Crystal wasn't feeling well. We didn't go to church. The day was just totally depressing.

So far today the prosecutor called me for a meeting on Friday. The lawyer called for a meeting on Monday. All I do is run downtown.

Decisions, Decisions

March 1st, 1991

Today started at 7 a.m. Crystal and I went to school at 8 a.m. I had a math conference with her teacher. Her name will be on the list to be one the first in September to receive extra help in math. At 9 a.m. Seth, Teri, and I went downtown. First, we met with the prosecutor till 11 a.m. He told us about what he is doing and why. He explained it all step by step. He is 99% sure Mark is going to plead guilty of felonious assault.

March 12th we will know for sure. Judge Tracy will also set a sentencing date on this day. I plan on being there at 9 a.m. Carolyn is going to go with me. I will also have Myra (women helping woman) there too. I am finally glad to see dates being set. It's about time. He's been sitting in that jail too long anyway.

I also decided to let Seth see Mark today. The prosecutor didn't want me to, but I have to put Seth's best interest at heart. Anyway, Teri took Seth to the jail at 11 a.m. Mark saw Seth from 11:10-11:40 exactly. Teri said that they laughed a lot. Seth said that Mark was shocked to see him, and he shook some, and they both were nervous. Seth didn't let any anger out on him like I thought he would. I was surprised he even visited the whole 30 minutes. While he was in the jail, I was downstairs waiting out the slowest 30 minutes of my life. Finally, Seth came down. He was fine. He didn't say much about it though.

We were about ready to leave when here comes two of Marks family members. She spoke to Seth. She asked me if I saw Mark. I told her no that I was not allowed to and I didn't want too! She went on in the jail. Marvin stopped to hug me and talk to me. I apologized to Marvin for not telling him I was bringing Seth down there. Seth had used all the visiting time.

We followed them up the hall and watched them get on the elevator. She was so angry we decided to wait for the next elevator. Even Teri said she had never seen anyone as angry as Thelma was. Well, I guess she will get over it all someday. I might as well face it; Thelma will be mad at me for life. I still pray for her though. She is still the kids' grandma.

(Actually, she did not stay mad at me. I visit her sometimes.)

At noon, over to counseling we went. I had a nice visit with her. She says I look more content this time, because I know a date has been set finally. She always makes me feel a lot better when I talk to her. We left at 1 p.m.

Decisions, Decisions

In the car Seth informed me that I was, "a selfish fool," because I wouldn't let Mark have his glasses. I lectured him good for saying this to me. He told me that he told his dad that I would give him the car if he would sign the house over to mom. Mark did not answer this! Seth also told him that I filed for a divorce too. Mark was supposed to have these papers served today. I will call Bill (my lawyer) next week to see.

Seth's anger once again comes out on me, instead of Mark. That's okay though, I am used to this anyway. I know that someday Seth will understand all of this. He's only 12 trying to be an adult. He has grown up so much the last 9 weeks. He still isn't the same son I knew before December 24th. His dad has messed him up emotionally, and also as far as how much Seth will love him again. Well, it's 2 a.m. I will stop writing for now.

Another Call from Dad

March 1st, 1991

Realize, these phone calls are from an emotional 8- and 12-year-old.

Crystal: call from OP, pencils

Mark: What color?

(Crystal explains)

Mark: School

Crystal: Math- division

Mark: Seth came to see me

Crystal: What you done

Nervous

Another Call from Dad

Afraid to see you

Mark: That's okay

Don't have to come down

Scary

Crystal: What's new down there?

Mark: Different food

Guard gave me a pop and popcorn

Crystal: You used to make us popcorn, not fun now

Sad, not good

Mark: Pray for dad, I pray everyday

Crystal: Book order

Principal book

Mark: Last letter with picture

Crystal: Copy machine

Which phone?

Mark: 10:30

Crystal: Mom said 25 minutes

Mark: How come?

Seth surprise

Crystal: Now you waiting for me

Mark: Okay

Crystal: I'm afraid of you

Mark: Okay, I understand

Crystal: Boots (her sat)

Pepper (our dog)

I wish you weren't there! I miss you a lot! Hard to tell how much.

Mark: You could want nothing to do with me

Crystal: Your brain snapped

Another Call from Dad

Mark: I guess that's one way to look at it.

Crystal: Why?

Mark: Just pressures

Crystal: I don't sleep, I get in mom's bed. I think about that night.

Mark: Bad, scary, be brave, forget about this, overcome this, pray to God to help.

Crystal: Nervous, about to cry! Not to cry to you.

Mark: Cry, it's okay. Hard on you, I understand. You'll be 9 soon.

Crystal: 12,13,15

Mark: People do a lot of bad things. Why do they? Not bad. Angry.

Crystal: Does it sound to you like I'm gonna cry?

Mark: Okay, you can cry.

Crystal: You don't care, you know why?

Mark: Um

Crystal: Basketball?

Mark: No

Crystal: Count baskets?

Mark: Okay

Crystal: Wish I could play basketball with you.

Mark: Me too.

Crystal: What else happen to me?

Mark: You get sweeter everyday

Crystal: I am the same

Mark: Counseling still?

Crystal: Missed because mom was at hospital getting her vest

Mark: Well

Crystal: Watch television?

Another Call from Dad

Mark: Yes, later

Crystal: Shows?

Mark: Bill Cosby

Crystal: Yea, funny

Skin, thumb

Mark: Don't let it get sore

Easter

Crystal: Shame, shame, no eggs for you

Mark: Yea, well

Crystal: Eat eggs for breakfast

Mark: Yea, maybe hard-boiled, and egg hunt

Crystal: I still have you Christmas present

Mark: Well, hang on to it

Crystal: I'm here and you're not

Mark: Well

Crystal: Do all prisoners go to church?

Mark: No

Crystal: They should!

Mark: Bible story about preacher in prison

Crystal: Let Seth talk

Mark: Okay

Seth: Hi dad

Mark: How are you?

Seth: You lied to mom, about the phone call, you told your lawyer

Mark: I didn't tell him what we talked about

Electric chair, 20 years

Seth: Maybe 20 years

Mark: Christians there, (3,000) prison!

Another Call from Dad

Seth: You were close to the Lord

Mark: Bible, pray, talked about church bad

Seth: Mom don't believe you are a Christian

Mark: Christians kill

Seth: Yea, I guess

Mark: It's bad, ran from the Lord

Bullheaded, God let this happen

He put me in position to make me turn to the Lord. God gets the glory. Not me, not mom. Joseph, David- order killing

Seth: Who killed?

Mark: Juanita knows

David, after God's own heart

Seth: He was punished though

I think you should be tortured; mom is.

Mark: Phone call

What punished

Seth: Not jail

Mark: Fire on me, make you happy

Seth: Yea

Mark: You would be happy

Seth: Yea, you have no pain though

Mark: I tell the judge to throw fire on me, not jail

Seth: Not enough!

Mark: Phone call, I'm hurt

Seth: Mom wasn't warned

Mark: People want to punish

Seth: Mom's position! Wouldn't you want them to be punished?

Mark: Yes

Another Call from Dad

Seth: Punished, right?

Mark: Not what I did, fear!

Seth: You broke the law. Would you be afraid he do it again?

Mark: Yes

Seth: Mom's pain

Mark: So, I should

I don't know

Pastor to wife

Put away for life

What else can I do?

Seth: Want you punished, but I don't

Mark: Law don't whip

Burn me and let me loose

I'm feeling pain, emotionally

Seth: Mom has that too, more

Mark: Have to hang up at 10:30

Seth: Your friend, black guy

Mark: Drug dealer

Seth: Do drugs?

Mark: Yea, his wife loves and forgives him

Seth: Mom wants to forgive you, and doesn't know how

Mark: Yea, I can understand that. Well, it's 10:25, I got to go. Put Crystal on.

Crystal: Bye dad. I love you

Mark: Hurry up! I love you

Seth: I love you, bye

Mark: I love you, bye now

10:30 (over)

Tell your mom I appreciate her bringing you down

You may notice that phone conversations with my children and their father becomes easier as the days and weeks pass.

New Thoughts

March 4th, 1991

I haven't written for a few days. I feel that my thoughts have calmed down for a few days. Now that I know a plea date has been set, I finally feel that things with Mark are being solved. After the March 12th date then there is the sentencing date.

Well, today Crystal told her counselor, Paul, that she is not happy. To her we can't be a happy family without her dad. I am going to have to work hard to show her that we can be really happy together. That we don't need Mark to be happy together. Me, Seth, and her can make each other happy. I am sure in time we will be able to manage this. I hurt for her because I am not sure how to show her that we can be a family of three. This is another question to turn over to the Lord.

It feels good to know that I finally received my first welfare check, also my Medicaid card came in. I am still waiting on the food stamps. I called all numbers to the bills I have. I sent some bills back with the Medicaid number

New Thoughts

on them. I used the Med-card to get my first prescription. I had my doctor call me in an anti-depressant. I have to call him back on Wednesday to let him know what I think. This pill can cause me to sleep, act silly, or constipate me. I am sort of scared to use it. My mom and Shonda seem to think I need it. I cannot get addicted though. I slammed the bedroom closet door (out of frustration) and a baby jar of coins almost hit me. Mark had two jars of coins hidden on the door ledge. Just another secret he hid from me. Later on, I will look for more money. I wonder if those coins were supposed to knock me out.

It is sad to know that the last year or so of my marriage was based on secrets, lies, mishaps, accidents, and so on. The things you find after someone hurts you and disappears from your life is shocking and hard to understand. What happens to a husband's mind that made him so mean, to do such a violent act? Will I ever know? Probably not, but I can try to understand.

Court Day

March 12th, 1991

Carolyn and I left at 8:15 and went downtown. We were in the courtroom at 9 a.m. We had to sit on the same bench as my in-laws. I let Thelma sit next to Carolyn, then me, and then Myra.

I sit there nervous, upset, and anxious to see what was going to happen next. Not a word was said to my in-laws from any of us. Nor did they speak. At 9:45 a.m. they brought Mark out into the courtroom. He glanced at me twice and struggled to have a straight face. Carolyn and I knew and could tell he was trying not to cry. He had to hold himself together to answer the judge's questions. He looked so scared.

The affectionate side of me wanted to hug him. The burnt side of me wanted to hit him and tell him off with a lot of anger. Finally, Mark pleaded guilty to felonious assault. Judge Tracy told him she could give him 5 to 15 years and a $7,500 fine.

Court Day

I am glad this date is over. Now there is one more date to get over with. This is sentencing day. Sentencing day will be April 9th. I left the courtroom and went downstairs to start a victim impact statement. The lady wrote down my incident. I also later will be sending another victim statement for Judge Tracy to read.

I went to Whalen's office and talked about a civil suit and other things. He felt I should have taken this to trial, but I am pleased this is a quicker way to get him into prison. A trial would have just drawn things out a lot longer. I am pleased with this decision. Mr. Whalen suggested that I go see Mark and ask him to sign all my papers (divorce, house deed loan, car, insurance).

My Visit with Mark

March 13th, 1991

At 9 a.m. Cindy and I left to go downtown. We are going to the jail, the child support office, and to see Mr. Whalen! At 9:45 a.m. we are sitting in the jail waiting for Mark to come to the visitor's window. Finally, sitting nervously, at 10:10 a.m. he comes out. I walked over to the window and picked up the phone. It took me a few seconds to look at him. He had tears in his eyes.

The following is what was said:

Me: I want you to sign the divorce papers, and the deed over to me, and income tax, and the life insurance. If you don't then I will file a civil suit which will include your car and you won't see your kids while you are in prison.

Mark: Why do you want a divorce so soon? (Something that he should ask.)

Me: Because it will make me feel safe.

My Visit with Mark

Mark: If I sign the house to you will that help you? Will you sell or what?

Me: I don't know, I am going to try to stay there. That is what the kids want.

Mark: I know that.

Me: The life insurance is just draining itself away. Sign so I can get the money.

Mark: Well, that's true.

Me: People who have seen you tell me that you have no remorse.

Mark: How am I supposed to show remorse?

Me: People have said that if you are truly sorry you will do what I ask. When I leave here, I am going to Whalen's office to give him your answer.

Mark: Do I have a choice?

Me: No, what is your answer?

Mark: Okay, I will sign everything you want.

Me: Don't say it unless you mean it.

Mark: I don't want a divorce, but I will sign the paper anyway.

Me: Don't tell Rubenstein and your dad until you have signed all.

Mark: I won't. Dad already told me to give you everything. He said you would win a civil suit anyway.

Me: That's right!

Mark: How are your burns?

Me: They are healing. The vest is a nuisance though.

Mark: Why won't Crystal come and see me?

Me: She is scared of you.

Mark: Are you going to bring them to the sentencing day?

Me: Yes, but I will not force Crystal to walk up to you. She has to do that on her own.

Mark: Okay, I know that.

My Visit with Mark

Me: Did you take my class ring?

Mark: No

Me: You have money hidden in the house?

Mark: Yes, above our bedroom closet door.

Me: I know, I found it, thanks for being honest with me. What made you think you could get away with this?

Mark: I don't know. I wasn't thinking.

Me: All I ever wanted was for you to love me.

Mark: I know!

Me: I have to leave to be at the child support office at 11 a.m. Do you want your old glasses? I have them.

Mark: Yes, give them to the guard.

Me: Bye, you can call me after you have signed the papers.

Mark: Have you heard of shock probation?

(Shock probation means that he would be released in six months.)

Me: Yes, but if you want me to put that in my impact statement, I won't make any promises.

Mark: Okay, just think about it.

Me: Okay, bye.

Mark: Vickie, I will never hurt you again.

Me: You can't guarantee that. You need mental help.

Mark: I know, I have told them.

Me: When you get to prison tell them, and make sure you want the help.

Mark: I know that.

Me: Well, I've got to go.

Mark: I'll call you later.

Me: Bye.

I gave the guard his glasses. He is only allowed one pair, so I brought his new glasses back home with me. Cindy and I wondered if Mark would keep his word and sign the papers. We went to the child support office where

My Visit with Mark

we had to sit for 45 minutes. At 11:45 a.m. we went to Whalen's office. I told him what Mark said. Whalen will serve the papers on Thursday for Mark to sign them all.

I was proud of myself. As scared as I was, I didn't cry at all. Mark cried a lot and he shook a lot too. He is really scared of going to the prison. I feel sorry for him. Why do I feel sorry for him? He set me on fire. Six months before that he choked me. For the past year he has been mentally tormenting me. He has lied, cheated, and hid things from me. I should hate him, but I don't. Maybe I need more time. Just maybe my feelings and emotions are all mixed up. Only time will tell. I will just have to pray about this also.

(Hebrews 12:14,15 Unforgiveness)

Signed All

March 14th, 1991

Today, I am anxiously waiting and praying that Mark will sign all the papers for us. At 9:20 a.m. the phone rang! It was Mark! I expected the phone call.

Mark: Why do you want a divorce? As far as I'm concerned, we will always be married. You have no Bible grounds to divorce me.

Me: Yes, I do! You claim you have committed adultery!

Mark: That was three years ago.

Me: You said you did a few months ago.

Mark: That was just a lie.

Me: I don't know that.

Mark: This divorce is on you, not me.

Me: I know!

Mark: You know the Baptist don't believe in fasting.

Me: Yes, they do, we just don't practice it. Did you do all the things that I called the police about?

Mark: No

Me: Well, how come nothing has happened since you left here?

Mark: I don't know.

Me: I don't know whether to believe you or not. I'm going to recommend that the Board of Corrections send you to Warren County Jail, so you can be close to here. It's a nicer jail too.

Mark: Okay, that would be nice. Will you keep my glasses for me?

Me: Yes. I am going to keep your bike and weights too. Seth wants them.

Mark: That's okay too. I've got to go.

Me: Mark, I don't want you to hurt and I do care about you.

Mark: I care about you too. Bye!

Me: Bye, see you later.

I feel so lonely and guilty about all of this. I know this needs to be; I just wish none of this would have happened. I just need to pray more. I feel so sad.

March 15th, 1991

He called again and ask me to bring his suit to wear on court day. He also asked me to send him a copy of the song *Neither Do I Condemn Thee*.

I am really upset! I am scared for him. I don't want him to get hurt. I still have feelings for him. I always will. He now wants me to believe that he loves me, a little late now. I keep asking myself, "Why did he do this to us? Why couldn't he just love me and be happy with us as a family should be? Why? Why? Why?" We will never know why! He is so afraid of going to prison. Maybe he should be.

Going to prison is what he deserves. He could have killed me. He could have burned our house down. He could have harmed his kids. Yes, he does deserve prison. After all, I don't want him to come after me. He needs a long time to think about what he has done to his whole family.

Signed All

March 17th, 1991

I am now sitting in the car at my in-law's house while my children are inside visiting with them. I told Thelma that my impact statement will be nice. I also told her that I talked to Mark and told him I will recommend the Warren County Prison for him because it is close.

At 5:30 p.m. I went in to get them ready for church. Thelma and I had a nice quiet conversation. She thanked me for not taking this to trial and she thanked me for the impact statement words. I hurt for her a lot too. I feel so sorry Mark has done this to her. All of her children have hurt her so very much. I now feel that a lot of her anger has left and maybe she doesn't blame me. She only wants to believe that Mark snapped, reality is he didn't snap, he was just plain mean.

Judge Tracy

My Impact Statement

March 17th, 1991

Judge Tracy,

I have had almost 3 months to think and pray about this tragedy. I feel that my children and I will never again feel safe. They love their father but at ages 8 and 12 they will never realize how serious this act with fire could have been.

My only request and prayer are that Mark be sentenced long enough for me to get rid of the fear, and after 14 years of marriage try to get on with my life without him. I have filed for a divorce and as hard as it will be I need time to work out all the problems this tragedy has created.

Since I have two young children involved, I feel that I should not request on the time my husband, their father, should spend incarcerated. Reason being, that my children cannot come back on me and blame me for any of the events that have taken place the last 3 months.

I pray that Mark will ask for mental help while he is incarcerated, so that hopefully after he is released my children and I will not have to live in fear any longer. I feel I will never know why Mark set me on fire. I am forced to wear a Jobst burns vest for the next nine months. I will for a long time have the scars physically and emotionally because of this frightened act on December 24th, which took me away from my children on Christmas.

Twelve jurors indicted Mark with felonious assault, and aggravated arson. I will pray for you as you make your decision about the sentencing of a man who performed such a violent act, and has destroyed his family's home life.

Respectfully,
Vickie Gibbs (victim)

Seth was asked to write an impact statement also. The following is what he wrote. He may be 12, but he is very smart and sensible. I was very proud of him:

Judge Tracy,

I feel what my dad did was wrong, very wrong for that matter. He should not have done what he did. I still love him, but it happened and there is nothing I can do. So, I really don't care if you give him 5 years or 25 years, so what I ask is that you give him whatever you feel is right! Dear, Seth

(Seth put his honest feeling about his dad in this impact statement.)

Crystal was also asked to make a statement. She may only be 8 years old, but she does have feelings. This is what she wrote:

Judge Tracy,

I don't think my dad is a bad person. I do wish he haven't done this to my mom. I am very unhappy, because of this situation. I am really sorry for my mom and dad. My mom is really upset about this bad situation. My dad is afraid of prison. I am afraid of my dad because of his looks. I miss him a whole lot, and love him very much. I wish he haven't of done this and then nobody would be very upset. My grandma Gibbs blames it all on my mom and I don't know why she does. My mom is missing my dad. She says if she could go down there where dad is she couldn't get him out. My mom was up all night last night. She talked to the pastor's wife and me and my brother fell asleep in my mom's bed, and then she got up in my brother's bed and fell asleep. Then I got up and laid down with my mom and fell asleep. Then my mom got up and went and laid in her bed with my brother and I fell asleep in my brothers bed the rest of the night. She was upset all night. This is all I can say for now.

Love,
Crystal

Unwanted Thoughts

March 18th, 1991

It's 6:10 a.m. I sit here listening to my children fight while they eat. I can't handle this. I am really in a state of mind not to handle this. I don't know why but I feel that I need him so much. I must be crazy, but 20 years (includes the years we dated.) of love can't be killed. Somebody help me! I have talked to Carolyn, Rose, and Diana. Nothing they say can help me. What am I going to do?

(You call tell my frustration is getting to me).

I guess I just need lots of time to find a job and get on with my life. Maybe someday soon meet a new man who will love me more than ever, and treat me like a queen. I need love in my life to fill all of my loneliness. I most likely have another sleepless night like last night. I saw a picture of him in my face all night long. I miss him so very much. Why do I miss him, I am not sure, but I know there was love there at one time.

DEUTERONOMY 31;8 (He will not fear you or forsake you.)

March 19th, 1991

Well, Mark called today. I talked to him and expressed a lot of feelings. Some I should not have expressed. I need to get all these feelings out in the open though. There is so much I want to tell him. A lot of this is anger, some of this is fear, some of this is love too, some of this is loneliness.

Seth finally told me that he misses his dad a little. I think he means a lot. Crystal is thinking about going to see him. She is still afraid. Mark wants me to talk to judge Tracy in person. I don't think I can do this though. Deep down inside I still want him to do at least 2 years. I need that much time to get on with my life. Really what I mean is I need time to stop loving him. It will probably take another man to cause me to lose my love for Mark. This is another need of prayer.

March 20th, 1991

I received a typed-up letter that Mark wanted me at first to sign and send in as my impact statement. Before I received it, he told me to tear it up. The words in this statement were a bunch of lies as far as I am concerned. I could not sign something that was not my feelings at all.

This is the letter I received:

The honorable Judge Ann Marie Tracy
Common Pleas Court
Hamilton County Courthouse
1,000 Main Street
Cincinnati, Ohio
Zip Code- 45202

Your Honor:

I send this letter in regards to my husband Mr. Mark. I was a victim of my husbands' desperate cry for help. He had a momentary setback mentally where all his systems of reasoning shut down. During the most stressful period of his life (as most humans do) he lashed out very unconsciously at the very person he loved and inflicted pain and damage.

Without excuse in most cases but forgivable in all if there's enough love and understanding. I forgive my husband for the pain and suffering inflicted on me. He's needed help and even now is suffering in a most traumatic way. I had a taste of hell for a few moments at his hands. But his are for longer periods in nightly remembering. He is now a victim.

I'm in some therapy and responding/readjusting well as can be expected. It takes time. I know Mark is seeking help and will follow through on the course of serious intent. I'm interested in and am willing to participate in any therapy sessions/treatments available to him that are inside or outside confinement available to him.

I love Mark enough to want to know what problems he has and how and by what means they can be resolved. I married for better or worse. This was but has now passed the worse. Mark wouldn't desert me. I will not desert him in his time of need. We can both help each other through this ordeal.

I believe love through being patient in helping Mark will prevail over all else with the proper therapy by needed professionals. I've 2 elements of love and being patient, I've spoken of as you can see. I'm visiting Mark now and will continue to throughout his stay, where ever he might be. I ask that you further consider, evaluate and weigh all I have said herein.

Mark does have many other outstanding virtues about him I haven't time or space to go into about. He is a worthwhile individual that there is room, time and many ways to save. If you would consider placing him under an in-depth investigation and look into the positive aspects of his life and listen to the up side of our relationship from me, I'd greatly appreciate it.

I thank you for your time taken in reading this communication and if I wasn't allowed to see you when I presented this letter in your courtroom, I am in hopes of be given an appointment to speak with you in the immediate future.

Sincerely Yours,

_____

Of course, I did not sign this letter.

I had to go downtown and pick up the life insurance paper from Whalen. Teri wanted to go with me. She did. I stopped in to see Mark. We had 50 minutes together. He looks a lot better than he did last week. He still is really scared about his sentencing though. The rest of the day was hard to face. My feelings are so mixed up.

When I got home, I had a card and a letter from Mark. Really sweet, loving letter. He's become a good writer with words. Too bad he didn't say all those things months ago. Well, it's hard to know how to take him now. This could just be a plea for help. Could be a butter me up letter, then the card was actually a card just to be friends someday. More things to pray for.

1:45 a.m. the phone rings! It's Mark! He was really upset. I talked to him till 3:45 a.m. to try to help him understand and to help myself understand. These phone calls upset both of us, but I feel to get over Mark we need to talk a lot of things out. It's something a man be in jail and supposed to be allowed to call this early in the morning. He is a porter so he gets extra privileges. This should not be, and it's unfair to the other inmates. Well, off to sleep.

March 22nd, 1991

Mark called at 8-8:30 p.m. He talked to the kids. He asked me a couple of questions. Carolyn was here. She even told Crystal to tell him "Hi!" After he called Crystal threw one of her fits. She was throwing Mark up at me. She needs to realize that throwing fits does not solve anything.

Mark wants her to see him. Carolyn and I tried to tell her that he looks the same. I want her to see him before he goes to Columbus, because if she decides to go then it will be too far to take her. I am going to take them Thursday to see him. I am praying she will speak to him. Well, we'll see!

I got out Mark and I's dating album to show Carolyn. This brought back a lot of old, good memories. I sorted a lot of extra pictures to send to Mark. The kids took some of them. At 11:30 p.m. Mark called again. I did not tell the kids. We talked till 1:15 a.m. and then we got cut off. I laid the phone down to put them in bed and came back and the phone was shut off. Mark warned me about this before. The kids tried to guess who I was talking to. I would not tell them, because they didn't need to know. He is calling tomorrow anyway.

Tonight, talking to him does not seem to bother me. Tomorrow it might. I believe my feelings are based on a day-to-day basis like all the problems I have to face. Seth told me he didn't want me to remarry Mark. He wants Mark to only see him on the weekends. He wants him out, now Seth says, "the only way Mark could prove himself to us would be to sacrifice one of his relatives." What an unusual thing to say. Just a feeling or thought to him, I guess. Well, its 4:20 a.m. I am going to sleep on the couch.

Seth is in the floor by the couch. Goodnight! I guess he wanted to be close to me.

March 25th, 1991

This morning I went to see Mark. When I walked up the jail steps, I saw Thelma and her friend Phyllis sitting there. I asked Thelma if she wanted me to leave, she said, "no". She said she would talk a few minutes and let me talk the rest of the time, and she did!

I told Mark what our pastor said. He was really mad! We had a nice talk for 50 minutes. I feel good when I talk to him. I talked to my counselor today too. She says I am in a detach stage. That seeing and talking to Mark is a way I need to break off with him. She has encouraged me to start job hunting.

Crystal's counselor says she should go see her dad. The window will not bother her either. She understands all of this too. She should be fine. When will all these mixed feelings stop and become a final decision that needs to be made? I guess with God's help only time will tell.

March 26th, 1991

Mark called me this morning at 8:40. Once again we had a nice talk. He was glad about what Myra and Crystals counselor said. We seem to enjoy talking to each other. I know what I say to him is sincere, but I still can't tell whether or not Mark is sincere with his words. He sure makes the words sound good. We had to hang up at 9:40 because he had a visitor. Sometimes this hanging up is hard to do.

I also got a nice letter from Mark. He can sure word things. Once again, I wish all of these words were said months ago. Now I am afraid no matter how much he writes, what he writes, cannot keep my feelings there long at all. Another matter of prayer. Everett (our friend) that our pastor is wrong. Everett agrees with the counselors. You can't keep the kids from their father. Well, this is all my decision to make. I have to do what I think is best.

The Big Day

March 28th, 1991

This morning we all got up at 7 a.m. at 7:30 a.m. we went downtown to go see Mark. This is Seth's second visit and Crystal's first. We were in the jail at 8:30 a.m. at 8:40 a.m. Mark came to the window. At this time, I said a few words. Crystal was standing behind me looking at Mark. Finally, when she saw that he was still the same she was ready to talk to him. Her and Seth took turns. After a few laughs and also mixture of words and 50 minutes he had to go.

We waited a few minutes while the guard brought me a bag of cards and things Mark wanted me to bring back home. We got outside and Crystal started to cry. She said, "daddy has been in there long enough and he should get to come home". She doesn't understand that our law has to punish him for what he did to me. Crystal said, "that the judge should know he has two children that is missing him". I tried to tell her that the law is the law and he has to do what the law says right now. I hurt for her because she really misses him.

Tonight, we went skating with the school and afterward we stopped and rented Robocop II. We watched the movie. At 11:30 p.m. I told Seth he had to go to bed. He got angry and back-talked me. When I went to tell him to be quiet, he slapped me on the arm. Well, I let him have it right back. I spanked his butt with my hand. I told him tomorrow he is to stay in his bed all day. I am going to stick to it too. He has got to learn that I am the parent and he is not going to back talk me at all and especially not hit me. (I wonder if he thinks it's okay to hit me because he saw his dad be abusive to me.)

I was one that never wanted to physically punish my children. Their father did enough of that. Now I feel I need to be firm or they will be so defiant towards me. I just want to make sure that I punish with thoughtfulness and never out of anger. It's going to be tough, being a single parent, but with God's help I am sure I will do just fine even with mistakes.

ENCLOSED IS A LETTER FROM MARK!

The Big Day

Dear Vickie,   3/28/91

Please, don't mind if I'm writing you again. After I sealed the last letter more came to mind that I wanted to say to you. Before I started this letter I was in the break room drinking a cup of coffee. My memory went back to the times you made me coffee & brought it to me. At that time I took for granted you bringing me that cup of coffee. It's times like those that really get me to thinking about you. My apologies go to you for not saying "Thanks dear" Right now I'm looking into the near future hoping that I can again have the opportunity to experience such a time.

Vickie, I owe so much to you that when we do get back together that I know I will have to work overtime to make everything up to you. At age 16 I met you. At that time our love began to grow. Through all the many problems we stuck together. Our love is very unique & like no others. Even through this I can't help but believe that our love is not dead. It is my goal with your permission to revive our love. I know in my heart that I still love you. And no one else can do for me like you have.

My apologies have went to you a few times & I'm not going to make myself a repeater, for it is my high hope that you are doing everything in your power with God's help to completely forgive me. I did not say to forget, but to forgive. Please, if you can with time of coarse consider to do so.

I love you very much like I said before. Now with these words I will be a repeater, of course unless you want me to stop. Just because I'm in here does not make me say this, but rather it is the absense from you. Since I've been away my thoughts have had time to come to their senses & I have discovered that within me I had feelings towards you like you would not believe. Vickie, my true love feelings are in reality there & they are the ones that you've always wanted, but was not revealed.

I want to love you like I've never done before. I want to make you very happy just by knowing that I can really love you, in the best of ways. I know I cannot be with you right away & I will be willing to see you in secret for a good long while before we even get back together. you'll be very glad you did. I understand that you will have to gain much trust in me & you will.

Let me explain. Vickie, my life before was all myself. You knew this & so does a lot of others. By being this way God was left out of my life & so was you. I'm not saying that I'm over my problems, but they are being chipped away. Realising this is a tremendous help & start. In order for you to be back with me you will begin my being my girlfriend just like in our beginning. Although in reality you are my wife. With the exception of God like I said before, I put them there so I must be the one to take them away. I'm really the only one that can. I'm very serious about this & I really mean what I'm saying.

Many times in my letters It may be found that I may say the same things. But please understand when I write a lot of letters I forget what might be in one letter. But some things will be repeat on purpose such as I love you because it is true. These repeats I hope you don't mind.

I have really been enjoying our phone conversations. Like you, it hurts when I hang up I miss you very much. I wish very much that I could be there just to talk with you or to just look at you. I also wish I could hold you in my arms for a while If I were with you right now I could probably hold you for a very long time It may be frightening to you, because of what has happened, but I would give you the best of comfort.

181

Dark Shadows

I really do appreciate the phone calls very much. Seriously when I heard your voice it gladdens my heart. Your voice has been a part of my life for 20 years & I w. your voice for 40 more years. I really do. So again thank you very much.

Sorry I cannot be with you for another holiday. I wish I could be with you. I also wish I could give you some type of present.

In just a few more days & I will be sentenced & may be leaving soon after that, at that time I will not be talking to you or seeing you much. This time will really hurt. Don't forget about me. If you have any love for me, please let it grow while I'm away. You must understand that I'm going to be lonely without you just like you will be towards me. I will be needing you more. While I'm in here at times I may be driven to think the worse. Please don't let my mind wander.

Each letter that I send you please take them to heart. I really mean every word that I say just like I said in the last letter. I'm going to write to you very often and would like to hear from you.

Right at this moment my heart is hurting for you very much. I need you to be with me. I really miss you very very much. I do want you to lose any love for me. Allow me to be near your heart. Keep me in your heart don't let ever get out. I belong in your heart & you belong in my heart. Years ago I can remember that we entered each others heart and said we would stay there forever. I want to stay in your heart.

Well love I think I will close this letter for now. I want this to get to you as quickly as possible. Again take this letter to heart. Believe every word.

Be mine dear & let your love grow for me. My love is growing for you. I want to help you in every way. I really do. Thank you again for receiving my letter.

I love you very much & I always will. I truly miss you very very much.

Be mine Forever
love

Back Home

April 6th, 1991

It's Saturday, April 6th. All in all, the kids and I had a good week in Kentucky. I tried my best to forget about Mark and the sentencing day. This was hard to do. Everyone talked about other things to help me. Our family sure has a lot of problems.

The worst thing about this trip is that on Thursday at 11:15 p.m. Mark called. Mom answered, she did not accept the call of course. This would have been .70 plus long-distance minutes. He had no business calling at mom's, especially the way he knows how mom feels. The best thing was being at Cindy's away from the kids a day and a half. I needed this too, really bad.

Here we are though. The kids are waiting for Mark to call. It's 10:20 p.m. and they are still waiting. They hate the waiting and wondering if he's going to call at all. After this week he won't be able to anyway. This will be hard on them, but maybe better in the long run.

Finally, at 11p.m. he calls. Both kids talked to him till midnight. Crystal wanted more time so he called back and talked till 1:30 a.m. It sure made her real tired too. Plus, tonight we lose an hour of sleep. These phone calls are nice for them, but sometimes can be upsetting for all of us. It's a shame any of this had to happen, but I'm sure the Lord has a lot of blessings in our future for us to endure.

AND HE DID

Back Home

Dear Vickie, 4/8/91

Thankyou very much for coming up to see me today. It really does mean a lot to me. I hope that you are here because you want to be here to see me as well.

Vickie, The tape that you will be hearing I sung for you I want you to listen to it as soon as you get it. From my heart to you it truly goes to you.

Tomorrow & tonight pray for us both. I will be praying as well. I will be nervous just as you may be. Without a doubt I will be in tears. But just remember there will be a lot on my mind at that moment, but I am consider each tear that I will be shedding will be soley to you. My mind will truly be filled with how much I really do love you & how much I'm going to miss you.

Do me a real favor, keep me in your heart every single day & every passing moment. Take me with you wherever you go & whatever you do. Keep your heart very fresh with me.

Another favor please, try not listen or be influenced by what others may say. Remember only you & I really knows what we want. I'm going to take you with me as my wife & I want you to let me return to you as your husband.

Please, through all of this try extra hard to believe that I love you very much. Don't grow cold towards me. Our love is not dead & I believe that our love is still very strong I just need to be there to show you

As soon as you get my address, write to me often. Send your feeling & yes, your love to me in those letters. Let our love grow more than it even has. It is there

Dark Shadows

and it can grow.

Always hold on to the hope that is there. Don't ever let go.

Very much I want to date you & redo the many things that we use to do. I realy believe that this would be very exciting. I want to wear something from you. If you will & would like give me something. This will keep my mind on your more.

Thankyou for everything that you have already done for me. keep doing for me in any way that you can...

I will write you soon.

I love you & I miss you.

Be mine for-ever & ever.

Love.

The Last Visit

April 10th, 1991

At 6:30 a.m. I got the kids out of bed. At 7:10 a.m. we left for downtown. At 8 a.m. we are in the jail visiting room waiting to see Mark. At 8:20 he finally came to the window. This was an emotional visit for all of us. We only got to talk for 20 minutes. Seth was sad and didn't talk much. Crystal was sad and talked a lot. I said a few words.

Next week, he will be moved! This will be especially hard on the kids! Another adjustment they need to make. We got out in the parking lot and Crystal cried. She doesn't understand all of this and probably never will. I pray with time she will understand and realize that God only puts on us what He knows we can handle.

Mark will be moved to a prison today. But first, he has to be processed

in Columbus, Ohio for six weeks. During this time there is no calls and no visits. (It's a safety rule.)

The Night Before

April 8th, 1991

Today I went downtown to take Mark his court clothes. I also exchanged them for his clothes that he was arrested in. I had a 25-minute visit with him. He is really troubled about his sentencing tomorrow. I still feel that the Lord will have a big part in the sentencing of him. I left him saddened. I feel guilt over all of this. Even though I know that none of this is my fault I intend to feel that I didn't do enough to help him.

I left from there and I ran a lot of errands. At 12:30 p.m. Mark called me. We talked till 3 p.m. This phone call was a need to help him deal with tomorrow. I feel that some of the things said in this phone call just proves that we could never live together again. There is still a lot of anger and resentment there about past things before this ever happened.

This is the 17th phone call since March 15th. I have allowed these because Marvin has paid for them. This week I am letting him call all I want because when he gets

The Night Before

to prison, he can't call. My feelings are so mixed up. I do not know what Mark should get. Little Crystal says 3 years. Seth acts like he doesn't care, but deep down inside I know he does. He is hurting and he just won't say!

I know they hurt, but I don't know how to help them. Well, it's 12:30 a.m. I guess I should go to bed and try to rest. Tomorrow is a turning point day for all concerned.

p.s. Mark signed his car title over to me today. This is another way of showing me he cares. Tomorrow I will have a lot more to write about. Until then! My prayers are on all of this.

The Sentencing 4.9.91

April 11th, 1991

It has taken me 2 days to gather my thoughts to write about sentencing day. Carolyn, Teri, and I left at 8:20 a.m. We arrived downtown at 9 a.m. We sit outside the courtroom on a bench waiting for someone else to arrive.

There appeared a Channel 12 newsman with a camera. I tried to get Teri or Carolyn to get up and ask him whose case he was going to report. They wouldn't do it, so I did! He said, "mine". Well, I quickly turned away. Shonda and Jeff arrived. We went into the courtroom and sit in the second row.

As we all sat, my nerves were anxiously waiting for Mark's case to come up. Finally, mom and Cindy came into the courtroom. I got up to sit close to mom. I saw four of Marks family members outside the door. Elzie kept looking in. Finally, they all came in and sat in front of us. Mark's aunt Gerine and uncle Roy were with them. Mark's aunt Gerine looked back at me and smiled four times. At this time, I didn't know it was her.

The Sentencing 4.9.91

The prosecutor asked me to go outside with him. He asked me if I wanted to make a statement. I said no. I asked him to request a contact visit with my children. I went back in and sat down and cried. I became emotional. My tears were hard to hold back. A million things went through my head.

Finally, at 10 a.m. they brought Mark into the courtroom. He didn't even look back at any of us. Judge Tracy called the court to order. Mark stood before her with the prosecutor. His lawyer made the defending statements. He spoke so low no one could hear him speak. It was like he was hiding something. The prosecutor spoke loudly and very clear to get his point across. Judge Tracy listened carefully to his closing argument. He was very good!

The courtroom was so quiet you could hear a pin drop. We all waited for the sentencing to begin. Judge Tracy first asked Mark if he had something to say. He began to apologize to the court and softly speak with a shaky voice. Judge Tracy told him she believed that he did this act purposefully and reprehensibly. She stated she was sorry to sentence him harshly for the impact it would have on the children, but he brought it on himself. Also, she stated that Mark's family was not to blame this on me. To tell my children that this was not my fault. She even stated that she wished she could tell them herself. She was stern in her words and full of words. She explained her actions with much concern also.

Finally, she began the sentencing. She gave Mark 7-15 years, and not to come up for parole till the 6th year. No appeals and no shock probation. Well, this stunned all of us. Mom even had tears. Thelma broke down in tears. Marvin hugged her and Elzie stood silently. I got up and rushed out of the courtroom. I couldn't believe my ears. I wanted him punished, but I never thought it would be a six-year sentence.

Everyone was so emotional. I couldn't help but feel guilty, but then we all know he brought this on himself. How was I going to tell the children? This chapter is now over. We all must accept this and go on with our lives. Him in there and me out here. The kids must understand why all of this happened this way. Once again, I hurt for them. Life for them too, must go on.

Telling the Children

April 11th, 1991

Crystal took this sentencing of 7 to 15 years hard. I counted on my fingers till her 17th birthday, to try to help her understand how long Mark would be in prison. She cried! Seth mainly acted like he didn't care. This is his way of hiding his true feelings. I know the anger will come later. He did state he hopes dad could come to his graduation. This is 5 years in the future to see though. Things must go on and life lives on.

At midnight this night Seth told his grandma (Marks mom) that life goes on, and time flies. The prison chaplain, Rick Anderson, also talked with Seth after midnight. Rick also talked to me to help me understand a lot of things. This now has to be a closed chapter in our book. We must move on to a lot of new changes.

Dark Shadows

Dear Vickie: 4-13-91

    I really appreciate you coming up to see me and I'm looking forward to seeing you again. Just knowing that you care & that you are still hanging in there for me is of great help. Let's both pray very much that God will keep our love alive. And too that it will grow stronger each day. I really want this to happen.

    I know your feelings are still being somewhat mixed, but how are you feeling towards from a few weeks ago? When I get to where I'm going will you please, express all of your feelings to. Don't leave anything out. Share your entire life with me, so write ~~and~~ it all.

    The time that is before us does seem very long, but hopeful it may not ~~be~~ that long. Being away from you will be very hard. My heart will hurt very much. I am really going to miss you.

    Vickie, I want to hold you for a little while. I want to to you in person that I love you very much. Since I can't please, take these words in each letter that I write and apply them to your heart. If your love seems to ever be fading fight hard & get rid of thought that you do not love me. We must both work very hard to keep the love. I really believe that ~~#~~ our love can survive. Please, work with me on ~~keep~~ping our love stronger & stronger.

    Please, come & see me as often as you can. Come every week. By keeping in physical contact it will help more to keep us together. By doing this we can hold hands and maybe eventually I can get a kiss from ...

Telling the Children

Let my words saturate your heart. I love you & please believe me. Love me back in every way. Don't let anything or anyone convince you otherwise. Search your heart & see the love that you really do have for me. Vickie, we've been together too long to just give up on each other. Lets stay together forever.

I know that your body is scared. Your scars on your body are beautiful to me. I want to love your scars and I want them next to me. Vickie, I really mean this. Like I've said before & I really believe this, I put all of this on you & I'm the only one that can really & complete, take all of this away.

Look back from the time that we first met. We've been through a whole lot. So much has been shared & there has been a lot of good. Why should we even think of giving up on our relationship? Things can & will get better.

Vickie, thankyou for keeping me in your heart. Let me stay there forever. I love you & I believe that deep, you love me & that it will always be this way.

Bye for now.

I Love you   Love

The Move

April 15th, 1991

The last few days I have let Mark call since he is leaving today. He wasn't sure what day this would be. On Sunday, the 14th he called to tell the children bye. They took it pretty good. Crystal cried some, because she misses him so very much.

I went to the jail at 8 this morning. To no surprise I was told Mark had already been moved. Nothing was left for me either. I was somewhat shocked. I now realized that he is gone, 2 ½ hours away, and I feel lost. I sure hope this feeling is gone fast.

I went on to my OWP meeting. Then, at 11:30 a.m. I saw my counselor. She helps me understand a lot of things. At 12:30 I went to the Justice Center to get his court clothes. He had taken them with him. I came home empty-handed, empty-handed with material things. Praying to be empty-minded of Mark and needing to realize that I have to start a new life without him.

The Move

I came home from downtown. I called Thelma to let her know Mark had been moved. She said, "I hope you and your family are happy!" Then she hung up on me! I understand when she just heard that her son is going to prison.

At 7:50 p.m. Mark called to give me his CRC inmate number, he only had 5 minutes. Seth ran and got Crystal. They said hi, just for a minute or so. I called Thelma to give her the number, nothing else was said. She didn't like it, because Mark called me first.

I wouldn't listen to all of this. Oh, and I told her that Mark and I were divorced as of February 17th. She didn't like that Mark didn't tell her.

Five minutes later, she called back to apologize for what she said. Crystal answered the phone though. She wanted to talk to me. I told Crystal to tell her that I would not talk to her again. Crystal did! She finally gave up and hung up. Well, this made Crystal cry, because I wouldn't talk to her grandma. I will never talk about any of this again with her. They are going to have to call me when they want the kids.

Well, once again this is just a lot I have to deal with. I will have to pray for my ex-mother in-law. She sure needs a lot of prayer. As far as I am concerned this is a closed chapter also.

May 7th, 1991

Dear Book,

I haven't written since April 14th! I have met a new male companion friend. He is caring, concern, and affectionate to all of us. We started with letters. Started speaking on the phone, then on April 26th we decided to go out on a date.

We went to Applebee's and a movie. We also went to his apartment. I had a really nice time too. He is so gentle, caring, kind, most of all very understanding.

He has made it very clear that he only wants a friendship, nothing more. This is best for both of us. Feelings are hard to fight. I guess we will take this one day at a time. He is so special. He makes me feel good with his words of compliments, and his laughter, and honesty. I feel the Lord sent him to me just to boost my self-esteem. He likes me being myself. We are a special couple.

May 14th, 1991

Dear Book,

It's 2 a.m. and today Mark is 36 years old, spending his birthday in prison. I am not feeling really sad at all about this. After all, he put himself there. I did not do this. I did let the kids buy him a card and send it. I do not want to mail him anything. Next week, I will mail him his first and last letter. This is the letter that I wrote and plan to send:

Mark,

This is probably the hardest letter I have ever written. Since this tragedy I have been through a lot of counseling. There will always be so many questions that I will never know answers to.

I can't help but believe that you actually intended on killing me that night. I also believe you know you did too. I found a letter you wrote that proves you threatening to kill me. I have also found out information why Judge Tracy believes you did this purposefully.

Mark, I know that even as much as I loved you, I know now that I could never, ever live with you again. I could never let you touch me again. I will always, no doubt, have to look over my shoulder when you get out.

All those times I prayed, "Lord get me out of this marriage." I feel like he did. I feel good about myself. I can be myself. I have peace I never had before. Seth and Crystal are even at peace too. I even see happiness in them now. They are learning to love each other. They are learning to respect each other too.

Mark, I intend to go on with my life. You need to do this too. I intend on finding happiness. When you attempted to kill me, you proved to me that you were through with me. Why you just didn't leave I will never know.

There is no easy way to tell you this. I DO NOT want you to write to me anymore. DO NOT ask to speak to me either. I cannot allow you to ever give me another minute of sadness.

I can just imagine all the things you are thinking right as you read this. Well, you think whatever you want. You can't hurt me mentally or physically anymore. As far as the kids go, I will let them visit you in prison as often as they wish. I will not encourage this though. You must realize that, concerning you has to be as their feelings appear. I will not make them do anything they don't want to do. You have to know that there will be weeks they won't write. Weeks they won't want to visit. I will not attempt to pressure them into doing something they don't want to do.

I AM NOT TURNING YOUR KIDS AGAINST YOU! ONLY YOU DID THAT! When I get a few more things worked out with my lawyer I will send all of your things to your mothers. By the way, you can have all of your things, even the coins. I feel that Seth does deserve the bike. He is planning on going on a 60-mile ride with Jeff in August. You need to leave him the bike. The thing you treasured most!

As far as Crystal goes, you tell me what you want her to have. There is a couple pieces of jewelry I am keeping, because I don't want the memory to be with you when you get out.

Mark, a part of me will always love you, but when I look at my burns, then I realize how you must have hated me. You hated me so badly that you did such an awful act to the mother of your children. I have to start a new life now and so should you. I know I can do alright and I know I can do all things WITHOUT you!

Because of our children I will attempt to be your friend. Friend in only you seeing our children though. Don't ever think you can ever be in my life again. You can't! I won't let you ever! Most likely this letter will not hurt you much. However, you take this letter, just remember: you burnt me, I didn't burn you! You took yourself away from your kids, not me! Now the four of us will deal with this one day at a time and I know we can manage to survive this ordeal.

Remember, do not write me, I'll just mail it back. If you have something to tell me, put it in Seth's letters. May God bless you and keep you well and safe!

-Vickie

As the days go on the kids don't mention Mark much at all. I think this has a lot to do with no phone calls and also Art. They enjoy his company. Arthur spends his time with them equally. They enjoy him, of course, I do too. Yesterday, I finally removed all of Marks things out of the bedroom. I even took the wedding picture and marriage certificate off the wall. Then, I cried a lot. Once again, I have to accept this too. Our marriage is completely over. I have kept busy today. I intended on keeping my mind off of Mark. My mind has been on Arthur all day. I just finished writing another poem for him. He is such a great guy, really, really special.

Seth has said nothing about Mark's birthday. Crystal went to bed wondering why he didn't call. She said it's unfair they don't let Mark call on his birthday. I am really glad I have accepted this and I intend on going on with my life to find happiness. Now I am concerned about finding a job. Having the strength and energy to take care of all I need to in the future.

I added a page later to Mark's letter. This is what I wrote:

May 23rd, 1991

Mark,

The first four pages were written to you on May 7th. I want you to know last Saturday on May 18th, the kids were at your moms. They will never be allowed to go back. She will never be allowed to keep them again. They were also crying and really hurt too. Your mom needs to wake up and accept what has happened to you. She has really hurt the kids, even Crystal doesn't want to go back. In June, the kids only will be visiting you. Last day of school is June 6th. When you go to Chillicothe let Seth know. Someone will bring them, but your mom will never be allowed to take them. (Of course, once again this was my anger speaking. I did let his mother take them to the prison to visit him.)

This is all, Vickie

It's Over

May 25th, 1991

Today my feelings are so mixed and assorted. Friday, I mailed the 1st and only letter Mark has ever received from me. Even though I have decided to shut off all contact with him I feel somewhat sad. I will never understand any of this.

As of Wednesday, I do know though that I know longer have any feelings for him. I have never been revengeful, but I do know he deserves to be hurt. There is still a lot of things to be settled, the car, kids visiting. Getting on with my life and being happy.

I know I can survive. The kids seem a lot happier outside of their fighting all the time. They are more peaceful too. The best thing out of all this is meeting Art or Arty to Crystal. He is kind to us. He is gentle, respectful, and shows much concern for all of us. I have made physically a new meaning though. Most of all he lets me be me.

It's hard to understand his definition of "friendship" though. He has different kinds of friendships with different friends. I don't even know if I'm allowed to call my friendship special to him. He is so special to me. He wants no relationship, determined to not fall in love, loves to travel. He may even be leaving this state next month for a new job.

I have tried hard not to, but I feel my affections are too strong, too soon. I knew going into this that we were only to be good friends, out to have a good time together. It's silly, but May 1st when he leaves for Canada, I know I'm going to miss him tremendously. I have no right to, but he is so very special. If I could have only met him 20 years ago. I pray that there is another guy as nice and as concerned as Art is. This will have to be another matter of great prayer.

June 18th, 1991

Tonight, was a time of hurtful feelings. Yesterday spent with Art was fun, great, and exciting. However, he says he can't handle the feelings anymore. Sometimes, he makes me think he is hiding true feelings for me, but he assures me he is not hiding feelings for me. I enjoy him very much. I feel that he is afraid of something. I'm just not sure what it is.

It's so hard for me to handle this thing of different kinds of friendship. Maybe, it will be best if he moves to Canada or Colorado. I don't know which is worst, this kind of relationship where there is no relationship or a relationship where all feelings of love move too fast, like rushing into marriage. Be my luck the next guy I date will fall fast in love with me and want to rush into marriage, and me not be in love with him. Boy, then what will I do? Maybe, I'll just stay single forever! My emotions are flying fast.

CHILLICOTHE PRISON

June 14th, 1991

Yesterday I managed to make a trip to prison. We were all scared. We didn't have to be searched. They only allowed me to take my license and my sunglasses in. They assigned us a table which we all had to sit together outside. Mark played with the kids. I had no trouble sitting and talking with him. He wished me the best with Art. He said he was glad the kids have someone to do things with. He didn't want a divorce. I didn't give him much choice.

Seth was bored the whole time. He kept saying, "I want out of this cage!" I ask him again why he couldn't give me an answer. He didn't receive my 5-page letter. (I am not sure I believe him.) We don't know why. He will never be able to give me an answer to any of this. I will always wonder why. He has accepted where he is v well, almost too well.

It was a joy to see Crystal run to him when he walked in the visitor's room! Seth just stood there. She was so happy. My feelings were so mixed up. I wanted to hold him, but was afraid, a part of me was mad at him, a part of me hurt for him, a part of me wanted to leave, a part of me wanted to stay. All in all, the visit was worthwhile. I told him mostly what my letter said. I am proud of myself; I had the strength to go through with this visit.

When we left at 4 p.m. Crystal and Mark were upset. I wanted to hug him, but knew I shouldn't. I didn't want to give him false hope. Crystal didn't want to leave. It hurt me to see her so sad. The visit there was a new experience for all of us. I have cried a lot today and am really depressed. I can't seem to get anything finished. Seeing Mark again has made me miss him and stirred up a lot of feelings.

I wish Art was here to talk to. He helps me forget about Mark. I miss him a lot. Art is a good friend, a good listener. I am happy to have him to talk to. He gives me a male outlook in this situation. In two more days, he will be home and he is going to get the biggest hug he ever had. I can't wait.

June 28th, 1991

Today, I am sitting at the park at 2:00 in the afternoon and have decided to write my feelings and emotions on paper once again. It has been a while since I last wrote. So much has happened. My life is changing. I have too much free time on my hands though.

Last Friday night, my mind and body were a total shamble. I was taken to Providence Hospital and had some test done. I begin once again taking the nerve pill. Right now, the medicine is a need, to help me relax and calm down.

On Tuesday the 25th I felt another attack coming on. I took a pill and this did help tremendously. There is so much going on in my mind that sometimes it's hard to sort all of my feelings. I began seeing Mark's friend, Dave. He is really sweet and nice to talk to. There is so much difference between Art and Dave. I don't know why I need to befriend a male. I just know that men give me a sense of confidence in myself and make me feel important.

Another Prison Visit

July 27th, 1991

I haven't written for a while. Yesterday, I felt a need to take Crystal to see Mark. Seth didn't want to go, and I didn't make him. He stayed with Karen all day.

We got to the prison at 9:45 a.m. They found Mark at 10:30 a.m. Crystal was very overjoyed. They played, talked, and laughed. She misses him so much. She needs him. She really loves him. My heart aches for her so much.

Mark and I still talk with so much tension between us. Just another reason I know we could never be together again. I told him again to quit writing me or I would not let the kids have their letters either. I don't know if he believed me or not.

We left at 4:45 p.m. Of course, Crystal wanted Mark to leave with us. Tears came to all three of our eyes. It was a long drive home. An extra hour because of construction. We stopped at Art's for a minute, but he was leaving. Not much was said, he did, on his own, give me a couple of hugs though. Right now, he seems to have time for everyone he knows except for us. I realize he is really busy. I'm glad he finally has a job. I sit here now with tears in my eyes from being so alone. It's 11:45 p.m., I just called Art, to say "Hi" hoping he would say when he would like to come over. He just said a few words and said, "He was busy still." I could tell he didn't want to talk, so I said goodbye.

When we got back from the prison, we all had a letter from Mark. When Seth got home on Saturday, I told him. He won't even read the letter. I don't know if Seth misses Mark and won't admit it, or if he has satisfaction knowing Mark is away. Seth did tell me later that he misses his dad a little, but still won't read the letter. This is okay. I see a lot of healing that needs to be accomplished on Seth's part. He is so bottled up and needs to open up, but it will take him a lot of time to realize the reality of all of this. Between, being lonely, Crystal missing Mark, and Seth being so confused and unhappy I don't think any of us will get through this for a long time. Just seems like God and friends are not enough. Crying doesn't even help. Our 15th anniversary would have been in 3 days and Mark is in prison. It's midnight, I should try to sleep.

Flowers

August 7th, 1991

I was amazed Sunday, because Dave brought me two dozen yellow carnations. It was a nice surprise. We went to his house and his church and enjoyed the evening. I feel I have to be comfortable with him. I also have to be careful. I sense he wants a fast, serious relationship. The affection I also want. A nice hug, and a simple kiss can be fun.

At 7:30 till midnight we were at Carolyn's for a house of Llyod party. Tonight, I stayed up late to write to Dave. The kids stayed up till 2 a.m. to write to Mark too. Surprisingly, Seth finally decided to write Mark a letter. He also made him a nice picture of (I love you) and stickers. I think Seth's finally forgiving Mark a little bit. I'm glad he finally wrote Mark a letter. Mark will sure be pleased.

Hocking Hills

August 20th, 1991

Yesterday on Monday we completed our Hocking Hills trip. We spent the night at a motel in Chillicothe. Today, we got up and drove about 7 or 8 miles to the prison. We got there at 10:30 a.m. Mark did not appear until noon. We only stayed till 2 p.m. Seth was restless. I was nervous, and Crystal was even ready to go. This was because she wanted to finish our small trip.

I told him I would never be back. I told him I would never forgive him either. Crystal's feelings are the same. Seth told him that he forgave him a little bit, but he would never be back unless I bring him. I could tell that Mark was hurt by all of this. I hurt for him too, but he should of never did this to us at all.

(All of the above statements were true. Seth and I never went to visit again. Crystal went with her grandparents to visit.)

Court Day for Divorce

August 26th, 1991

Well, this is it. Divorce court day. Carolyn is there with me. We get there at 8:30 a.m. At 9 a.m. we noticed my name not listed on the docket in the hallway. Here comes Whalen, because of a property hearing, my name is removed.

Whalen had an affidavit in my file showing no need for a hearing. It is not expected, also no notice was given. I am very upset! Now it will take months to get back on the docket. I guess I'm not supposed to know the why to this. I am very frustrated though! I would like to see us divorced by November 24th, Thanksgiving, or especially by December 24th, which will be one year since this happened. Only the Lord knows when.

Still No Answers

September 9th, 1991

Yesterday was Grandparent's Day. I finally decided to let Crystal go see the Mark's parents. On Saturday night she called Thelma. Thelma told Crystal she was sorry and cried. Crystal was happy she got to go see them. I didn't like it though. When I picked her up, she said no questions were asked, and that nothing was said about me. This was a real relief.

Today, I saw my lawyer again. He still doesn't have a court date. Waiting is so hard! Mark called this morning. I did not accept the call. I told him on the 20th and that is what I meant. He will have to learn to do what I want, besides his phone calls only upset all of us and complicate things too.

Thoughts

October 7th, 1991

Finally, on October 3rd, I received a phone call from Whalen. My new court date is October 30th. I am somewhat thrilled, but I have to tell myself I will believe it when I see it.

I am going through a thought pattern. This is tough!

Deep inside I still love Mark. A part of me believes Mark loves me. I know this is crazy, but I must come to my visual senses and realize what this husband of 154 years did to me and our family.

Then, there is Art, so hard to understand and confuses me greatly. After speaking to him last night after 3 months of not hearing from him, I know now, and understand why he hasn't contacted his friends or family. My feelings towards Art are more than friendship, but less than in love with him. I just feel that he is so very special to me. As the first man I met after this crime, Art made me feel important and that there are men out there who do treat women like queens.

Even though Art only wants a friendship, I still feel that I can talk to him about anything. He has the positiveness that I need. His advice gets me going and gives me courage without telling me what I should or shouldn't do. Yes, what family says and what church friends say mean a lot to me, but Art was the first man to get me to realize that all men are not abusers. Of course, Women Helping Women helped me get through most of the guilty feelings I had. Art helped me realize it was okay to see other men.

Now, I'm seeing Dave. In this relationship I have to carefully keep my feelings intact. Dave wants more than a friendship; he wants a serious relationship. I constantly make it clear to him that all I want is fun and male friendship. What troubles me is that he may end up being hurt. I tell him always that he needs to see someone else, because when my divorce is final, I intend on seeing other men. This is a desire of mine, not a necessity. I am just determined to make sure the next guy I fall in love with will be the right guy. I do not intend on being alone the rest of my life. I am finding out that falling in love is one of the hardest things to do, to deal with and find out.

Finally Divorced

November 2nd, 1991

Wednesday, October 30th, I was in court. I haven't been able to write yet, because I have had 3 days of mixed feelings. The divorce went fast and my answers, to the few questions, were short and fast. Carolyn's there too. I haven't felt any relief. After all, he's been gone 10 months anyway.

I do believe that my feelings are still all mixed up. As always, a part of me will always love Mark and always want him. I realize this is hard for a lot of my family and friends to understand. There isn't much to say except that its just a piece of paper from the state. Probably, emotionally, I will always be married to Mark Dwayne Gibbs.

Counseling Crystal

November 4th, 1991

This evening has been a terrible evening. I have lectured Crystal and talked with her about school and behavior until I cry myself to sleep. She had a crying spell about Mark, that I could not console. Finally, she called grandpa Gibbs and he made her feel better. She still ended up crying herself to sleep though. I guess I'll have to let her go see him. When Elzie and Thelma go after all. This may help her from missing him so much. I try to do my best by my kids. Sometimes its so hard though.

VISITS

November 19th, 1991

Tomorrow will be 3 weeks since I was in divorce court. I still don't have a final paper yet. Dave and I both decided to quit dating and just be friends. He wanted to become too serious too fast, and I didn't. I know he is hurting.

Saturday, I talked to Art. He's really busy and worrying about his health too much. He said he would try to see me this weekend. It sounds like he stays under a lot of stress all the time. I really miss him a lot. I need to hug him. We'll see!

Well, Sunday I'm going to let Crystal go to see Mark with her grandparents. I hope it's not to upsetting for her. She is nervous. I'm scared to let her go, but it's been 3 months. She needs to see him. I'll pray about this. I know I can handle whatever reaction she gives me when she gets back. I love her very much, and I hurt for her. I don't want her to resent me for not letting her see him. After all, it's not my fault, or hers, Mark is in prison. Right?!

SADNESS

December 6th, 1991

I didn't write Thanksgiving night. I couldn't bring myself to write at all. So, now I can put my thoughts on paper. Also, it seems that time flies, I don't find time to write. My days seem exhausting, even when I don't write, they been put on paper.

Finally, this week I got to work at Taylor Elementary School for 3 days. Yesterday, I finally got to stop therapy on my arm. Monday, the decision will be made about my hand.

Thanksgiving night I spent the evening in tears. Much of my tears were memories and loneliness. It's ironic, but sometimes I feel that all of this has been a non-stop dream. I wish I could be a little bird watching Mark in prison.

It's odd, but today Seth read his letter and said, "He writes like a lunatic." I guess he is implying that his dad is crazy. His letters seem to change concept a lot of ways. Monday, Seth got the flu and has been home all week. Tonight, Crystal has started with a cough and fever. It's always something. I never realized being a single parent was so hard. I do realize that there is lots of single parents out there in the same situation I am in.

Christmas 1991

December 30th, 1991

Let's see, we got through Christmas with mom on the 21st. We got through Christmas Eve day, although Crystal had some tears with the thoughts of her dad not being here. We got through the determination of putting up a tree, wrapping presents. Winterfest with the church, and the Festival of Lights at the zoo with Carolyn. The kids went to Thelma's for Christmas on the 22nd.

Christmas morning started with a confused, disconnected phone call from Mark which upset Crystal. After that, Christmas was great. I took lots of pictures to make up for last year. (A memory of being in a hospital and not with my children because of what their father did last year on Christmas eve. Seth and Crystal were both quite pleased with Christmas. Their smiles were a blessing in them to see. Seth even stated that this was the best Christmas he ever had. He was well pleased, especially with his Christmas present from Karen and Steve, they gave him lots of baseball cards! I was thrilled to see his joy.

Christmas 1991

Christmas night, we went to church to have candlelight service. It was great. Seth went home to spend the night with Karen. I didn't want him to go, but I wanted his Christmas to be what he wanted it to be. Katie stayed the night with Crystal and I. This was a great Christmas and, all in all, understandingly day even without Mark's presence.

On December 26, at 8:30 p.m. Mark called. I felt the need to talk to him so I did. I needed to know that he was okay. He says he makes the best of it. It was a relief to speak to him. I do care about him still. A part of me will always love him. When the 10 minutes was up, I let him call back to talk to Crystal. She was thrilled and excited. The time goes so fast. She never gets to say all she wants to. I hurt for her, but I can't help her.

It's really unique! Maybe, it's loneliness, but we have done more this Christmas as a family of three, than we ever did with Mark here. Christmas Eve, we went to Jeff's church. Then, to Shonda's for snacks. Seth and I stayed up till 6 a.m. Christmas morning wrapping gifts.

On Saturday the 28th we went with Carolyn and Ricky to Adams County to see the 40-acre Rudd family lights. Mark wanted to do this for 3 years, but we never did. Crystal was at moms from Friday to Monday. The drive to the lights was worth it. The lights portrayed the family of Jesus and the story of His birth through Easter.

Monday, the 30th, I took the kids to Sawyer Point and Fountain Square to see the lights. This was fun too! We have done everything possible to do this Christmas. We made this Christmas great, and with the grace and faith of God it was the best!

New Year's 1992

January 2nd, 1992

New Year's Eve we went to our pastor's house. We played charades and the outburst game. It was a lot of fun. People present were friends from church. I enjoyed celebrating with my Christian friends. At midnight, we all including the kids had circle prayer and gave testimonies till 2:30 a.m. From 2:30 a.m. till 3:30 a.m. I helped the pastor's wife clean the dishes and we played Bible trivia.

We got home at 4 a.m. on New Year's Day. The kids and I had our traditional eggnog and prayer circle. Of course, I couldn't bring myself to light any candles. I don't like seeing the flames, just makes me nervous. I couldn't sleep, so I stayed up till 6 a.m. and wrote a poem for Diane and Teri.

Christmas and New Year's Day was great. I expect an even better year for 1992. My house is paid for. I desire to find a good job and to start a monthly Bible study with my friend, Kim. Our church will grow and be blessed.

Dark Shadows

A letter to Mark from Nathan.

Dear Dad

Jan. 12

How are you? I am doing very well. I did get a lot for Christmas. I do not want to name them all because I might be coming up soon. I will name the top things. I got the nintendo tape Ninja Gaiden, I got a hand game, I got a skateboard, I got 50 dollars from Grandma Collins. With that 50 dollars I bought a Bulls hat, a Buckey hat, book bag, nintendo tape called Tiger Heli and that is it. I still got some money left over. Other things I got from my mom was an Ohio State Buckeys sweat shirt and sweat pants that match, I got a bunch of baseball cards, I got a micro machine train that makes sounds. I got some more fish. I got 3 tiger Borb and I had a fiddler crab already. Dad I liked the

New Year's 1992

picture but I am getting a little to old for Turtles. I did like the ~~farfeild~~ Farfield. Dad will you draw me Bugs Bunny. I have enclosed some drawings. I hope you like them. I am still doing good in school. I am keeping all your letters in the folder you gave me. The one with the turtles on it. I got ~~a~~ some candy and gum in my stocking. I had a good Christmas. Dad draw me another picture of Bart. ~~Well~~ Dad I love you very much and I am sorry I ~~wrote to you a little late~~ didn't write to you sooner. Have the best time you can and I might be up there soon. This is all I have to say, so goodbye for now.

Love

Dark Shadows

A letter to Mark from Crystal.

1-24-92

O. Daddy,

I will come to see you Sunday Feb. 2. I can not wait to see you. I hope you will be ready for me, because I am ready for your kisses and hugs. I'm so excited to see you. I just can't wait. Did you know you are the best dad anyone could have? I love you more than words can say, so please be the best dad you can be to me. I have in my mouth ~~two~~ two spacers, 9 feelings, and a crown and I also got my teeth cleaned at the dentist. Nothing hurt but the shot, the shot stung a little bit. I hope God is answering our prayers because I keep praying & praying that god will get you out of jail so ~~on~~ we can be together again. You are doing a good job writing these letters to me. Will you please draw a picture of Boots on a card, her eyes are green, her fur is black, and white, she has a pink nose and will you please draw me a picture of Pepper? She is gray & white and she has a brown nose but please do these pictures of Pepper & Boots on a card when you have time to do them.

New Year's 1992

I am sorry we are apart, and not together. But do not worry because I will be there Feb 2, 92, with G. & G Gibbs, it will be fun to see you. Well, I will go now because I have nothing else to say, but there is one thing I forgot that is important to me and you and that is I love you and miss you very (18 times) much.
                    Love, Your Plum

Letter to Mark

March 4th, 1992

Mark,

As of November 1, 1991, we were divorced. I received the papers today. Here is your copy. Feels relieved to be somewhat free. Free of you, but not free of the scars you have inflicted on my body, physically and emotionally.

I once believed you loved me, but since you have been in prison, I now know you don't and never did. For instance, your belongings you have received while in prison you have sent home with your mom. Not me!

If you loved me, you would have wanted all of your cards, letters, whatever sent to me, not to your mom's house. Then, you always were secretive about everything. Now, I don't care! Like Art tells me, you are as if you were dead, as far as I'm concerned. You took yourself away, you caused our divorce, you hurt our kids. Only you destroyed the family you once had. What you do is your concern and mine is mine.

As of next week, your clothes and some items will be taken to your moms. I have had them boxed and in storage since February of 1991. Now that I have the divorce papers, I'm ready to get rid of your things. I've had a lot of suggestions of what to do with them, but I'll be nice and let your mom have them. I will send you a list of exactly what will be sent to her. Keep in mind I don't have to give you anything. Most of the things I am keeping are for your kids. They deserve the items, not you!

The church received your letter, and was posted on the backboard. I got a letter from Chaplain Charles Edgington. I will be writing him a letter soon. This is the last letter you will receive from me.

Goodbye, Vickie

Son's Visit

March 7th, 1992

On January 17th, Seth and I traveled to Chillicothe to see Mark. He was very surprised to see Seth. Seth hadn't been there since August. Mark still has that, okay, secretive, I'm great, stupid attitude. I did my best to ignore him and walk away as much as possible. He frustrates me so much. He still hasn't accepted that we are finished.

Finally, on February 28th, I received my divorce papers. According to the papers we have been divorced since November 1st. I guess I feel relieved, I'm not sure though. I still don't seem able to depart with Mark's clothes and other things. On March 3rd, I received a form to fill out for an inmate/marriage seminar. This surprises me, then on March 6th, I get a letter from Mark saying that he already sent the $80 to cover the amount of the seminar. I don't know how he got the money, but he actually thinks I would come! Well, on Monday he should be getting the divorce papers.

16 Months Past

May 26th, 1992

It's been 16 months. It's now May of 1992. Ever since December of 1990 I have been looking for a reason, a why, an answer to what Mark so cruelly did to this family. The closest answer that makes sense comes from Dr. James Dobson's book, Love Must Be Tough. I quote:

> A sudden outburst of sudden behavior is likely to occur anytime a more passive approach has consistently failed to ease the severe pain of inferiority.

The above statement Mark always claimed to be passive and to have an inferiority complex. It says a lot, but what do you expect? All of this was held in until he couldn't stand it, so then he planned a way of letting it all out, by setting me on fire. Then, even if this is why he hurt me, we will still never know why he chose such a cruel way to do it. A regular divorce would have been easier and a lot less complicated.

Over and Gone

May 29th, 1992

I finally did it!!!

Yesterday at 4:30 p.m. Seth loaded up all of Mark's boxes and I drove to Thelma's frustrated and upset. I pulled up on the edge of the yard and unloaded all of the boxes. I put the saxophone on the porch and knocked on the door to let her know I was there. She knew though, because she was peeking through the window.

Finally, she opened the door and asked me if I wanted something. I ignored her and got back in the car. She yelled thanks, and I drove off. I had on my sunglasses so she couldn't see my frustrated face of tears. I was mad, sad, and glad all at the same time.

Seth and I were in the shed and he threatened to burn all of Mark's things. I guess him saying this, Sunday's abuse article, Aunt Charlene's talk on Sunday, and my new special friend, Bill all together prompted me to take this final step.

(Yes, you read it right, my special friend Bill, Art and Dave are history.)

I know that a part of me will always love and remember the good times that Mark and I had. The memory of and knowing what he did to me and this family on December 24th, 1991 will always take far more preference over what love and feelings I once had for him. I know I will never forget and may never forgive him for such cruelty. I know my heart aches and I must go on and try to find a new life of happiness, single, or remarried, whichever is the Lord's will for my future and my children.

Let me end by saying, that I try to pray daily and thank God for the tremendous blessings God has given my family". I have learned that God does answer prayers, and with enough faith in God's time he does give us strength to get through whatever trials we have to face.

> God is ever-caring,
> God is ever-sharing,
> God is great!

July 1st, 1992

It has been a while since I wrote, but I'm excited today! My vest came off today and I'm really glad about this. No more tightness. It feels great not to have to wear the burns vest anymore. I still have to contend with either wearing long sleeves or showing the scars to everyone I come in contact with.

My feelings are uncertain about this. They don't look as bad as I think. It's just an emotional thing I have to cope with. Like everything else this all takes time and encouragement from good friends too. The scaring is about as bad as it will get. What's there now, is what will always be there. The redness may leave, but the scar tissue is there to stay. I might as well face it; Mark has scarred me emotionally and physically for a long time to come. I'll just pray about this and God will help me. He's a great God. Mark was sentenced to six to fifteen years without parole for six years. During his sixth year of imprisonment, I went to the Columbus parole board and suggested for them not to let him free. They did not parole him.

Mark actually served nine years. The parole board called me and wanted my thoughts about him being paroled. This was October of 1999. I told them that they could release him. My daughter wanted him at her graduation in May of 2000.

RELEASE THOUGHTS (Written in 1999)

As soon as I thought my life was happy and content, I received news that Mark was going to be released from prison. My fears were unexplainable to everyone that knew me. I wondered how I was expected to feel when the man that tried to kill me would soon be a free man after nine years of incarceration. My fears of him being free to do as he pleased, and come and go as he wanted was almost unbearable. I felt like we were switching places, and I had become the prisoner. I felt like I was always looking over my shoulder and wondering if he was watching me. I had fears that only a victim of such a horrible crime would ever understand. Only the Lord knows if he will ever make another attempt to harm me. I have had to learn to trust God and put my fears aside and continue in faith. I have realized that I am both a victim and the prisoner because the real prisoner was set free.

My advice to give other victims is to remember that God only puts us through the trials that he knows we can handle. We know that his a gracious, loving, and caring God. He will always be there as long as we have faith and believe and trust in him.

HELPFUL BIBLE VERSES

PHILIPPIANS 4:13

MATTHEW 11:28 (We are not to bear our burdens alone) (Give them to God)

PSALMS 68:19, I PETER 5:7 (Replace your burdens with forgiveness, healing. and restoration. Burden God with what burdens you.)

HEBREWS 11:1,33,34 faith, believing in God's character, Believing in Gods promises)

MATTHEW 11:28

YEARS TO COME

There's a time when you have to forget life trials and troubles. Go on with your life and live life to the fullest. Be happy and make the best of life.

Then I began to wonder if Mark will ever attempt to finish that tragic night in 1990. Will he go on with his life and forget about me? During his incarceration and years past hopefully, he will want a new beginning also.

I pray that as a free man he will enjoy his freedom.

It's been 32 years since that tragic Christmas eve. With the grace of God and support from family and friends my life has been a continuous blessing. Since Mark's release in 1999 I have saw him at my daughter's wedding, a funeral of a friend, a birthday party and my drought's 40th birthday celebration. My uncomfortable feelings were in God's hands. The attendance of these events was not about me but about the loved ones that were involved. God has always protected me and I refuse to live in fear. (Joshua 14:27) (Deuteronomy 31:8). No, Mark has never tried to see me or contact me since his release. I have always refused to live in fear of anyone or anything.

Now thinking back after our children were born was when we had problems. The attention given to Seth was too much for Mark. I told myself that things would change. Then Crystal was born. Things did change. Crystal was Marks pride and joy. She got most of the attention from Mark. I believe Seth felt unloved by Mark. I starting seeing our problems increase the following years. I saw a difference between the way Mark showed our children. This caused a lot of anger between us. Mark started being verbally abusive and dominate towards me. then he would throw and break things.

WHY DIDN'T I LEAVE?

I always heard "what happens in your four walls stays in your four walls."

"You made your bed so lie in it." "If the shoe fits wear it." Afraid of where to go. Where would my finances come from? How would my children feel without their father around? If I had known what the future would bring maybe I would have left.

A New Beginning

I want to talk a little bit about what has happened to me and my family since that tragic Christmas Eve in 1990. On October,8, 1993 I was blessed to marry again to a wonderful Christian man. We were in love and very happy. Little did I know again that my life would change so desperately. Six months after we were married, we found out that he had melanoma skin cancer. The Lord took him home thirteen months after we were married on November 4, 1994. As sad as this was for me and my family our lives had to move forward.

God is so great and wonderful. I received another blessing. I joined the widow, widower's group at my church where I was blessed again. There I met a man and we started dating and fell in love. On January 10, 1996 we were married. To this day we have been happily married for twenty-five years.

I will not mention my children's lives except to say they both went on with their lives facing a lot of changes. God has blessed them greatly to this day.

THE END

TO ALL WOMEN OF DOMESTIC VIOLENCE,
THERE IS HELP:

DOMESTIC VIOLENCE HOTLINE: 1-800-799-SAFE

COMMUNITY POLICE DEPARTMENT

FRIENDS AND CHURCHES

JUST ASK ANYONE-THEY WILL FIND A WAY
TO HELP YOU

GOD BLESS ALL.